A Psychodynamic Approach to Education

Alex Coren initially trained as a social worker and worked in the London Borough of Hackney and as a psychiatric social worker at The National Hospital for Nervous Diseases, London, and Camberwell Child Guidance Unit. After training as a psychoanalytic psychotherapist with the British Association of Psychotherapists, he worked at King's College, London, in the student counselling service. He has worked extensively as a counsellor and psychotherapist in secondary and higher education, both in the public and private sectors, and has contributed to teaching and training both at Birkbeck College, London, and in Oxford. He is currently Deputy Head of the University of Oxford Counselling Service.

A PSYCHODYNAMIC APPROACH TO EDUCATION

Alex Coren

sheldon **PRESS**

First published in Great Britain in 1997 by
Sheldon Press, SPCK, Marylebone Road, London NW1 4DU

ACKNOWLEDGEMENTS

Extracts have been reproduced with permission from the
following publications:

W. H. Auden, 'Letter to Lord Byron', in *Collected Poems*, Faber
and Faber, 1938

John Donne, 'Progress of the Soul', in *Complete English Poems*,
J. M. Dent Ltd, 1994.

We would like to take this opportunity to thank those
individuals and organizations who have given us permission to
use and adapt material for this book. Every effort has been made
to trace the owners of copyright material, though in a few cases
this has proved impossible and we apologize to any copyright
holders whose rights may have been unwittingly infringed. We
trust that in the event of any accidental infringement, the owners
of the material will contact us directly.

British Library Cataloguing-in-Publication Data
A catalogue record for this book is available from the British
Library

ISBN 0–85969–764–9

Photoset by Deltatype Ltd, Birkenhead, Merseyside
Printed in Great Britain by Biddles Ltd, Guildford and King's Lynn

| *Contents*

| *Acknowledgements*

I am greatly indebted to the large number of students and teachers who helped me towards an understanding of what studying might entail. This book is dedicated to them.

The original idea for this book arose from conversations with Adam Phillips. I thank him for his continuing encouragement and the enlightenment our conversations bring.

I would like to thank my colleague Elsa Bell for her generosity, encouragement and support.

The fact that this book appears at all is due in no small measure to Helen, Ben and Sam, to whom I would like to express my thanks for their sound advice, and who willingly suffered from my distraction and preoccupation during the writing of this book.

| *Preface*

I shall recall a single incident
No more. I spoke of mining engineering,
As the career on which my mind was bent,
But for some time my fancies had been veering;
Mirages of the future kept appearing;
Crazes had come and gone in short, sharp gales,
For motorbikes, photography, and whales.

But indecision broke off with a clean-cut end
One afternoon in March at half-past three
When walking in a ploughed field with a friend;
Kicking a little stone, he turned to me
And said, 'Tell me, do you write poetry?'
I never had, and said so, but I knew
That very moment what I wished to do.

W.H. Auden, 'Letter to Lord Byron', 1938

This book is the result of what I thought were random musings on the subject of psychoanalysis and education, which have been two of my interests and preoccupations during much of my adult life. While I was engaged in writing, and concurrently working as a psychotherapist in secondary and higher education, I became aware that these two preoccupations were not solely confined to the years spent as a so-called grown up. As a child I vividly remember the experience of being 'weak at maths'. This affliction led me to have to separate from my friends and classmates during mathematics periods and join what was universally, if informally, acknowledged as the lowest 'set' – although it was perversely called the 'A' set – and struggle with equations, geometry and even logic in a subject that seemed not only to be totally bereft of any reason and defy my comprehension, but also evoked in me the illusory quality of a dream: I was invited into a not altogether pleasant world, devoid of any apparent meaning, where things happened randomly and haphazardly, whose only ostensible purpose was to highlight my own shortcomings and humiliate me. It was the one period during the week when I felt I had left home without remembering to put my trousers on. I always hoped that one day I would wake up. It was only with the hindsight of adulthood that I began to understand why it had been so difficult for me to 'add up' and 'take away' at that age.

This book is about our subjective curriculum (Jones, 1968). In education one is continually involved in negotiation with one's early environment. Our personal and private scripts or agendas may be very different from the demands that education may make on us. Educational obstacles may be instrumental in telling us something of value about ourselves, and, like psychological symptoms, may need to be decoded. This book attempts that task.

Psychoanalysis and education may appear uneasy bedfellows, but they share similar histories. Initially radical theories of cultural and personal liberation, both are increasingly in danger of becoming ideologies of cultural adaptation and conformity. Psychoanalysis, in its origins associated with desire and its obstacles – that is, what we want and cannot allow ourselves to have – has become increasingly preoccupied with matters of nurture – what we think (or more frequently, what others tell us) we need. It is the contention of this book that education has always struggled with a similar dilemma, and is undergoing a similar transformation. Do we want it, or do we need it? The transition from what we want to what we need has involved both psychoanalysis and education in moving from curiosity and pleasure to compliance and submission. In the process something of value – our personal scripts and pleasure in our own confusing complexity – is in danger of being lost.

The initial hope and claims made for (and the eventual disappointment in) education as an agent of social change or transformation complement in their grandiosity early psychoanalytic writings on education, with their recommendations that all classroom teachers be psychoanalysed before being 'allowed' into the classroom. Hubris and omnipotent grandiosity, in evidence in both the history of psychoanalysis and education, has turned into excessive self-preoccupation and regard. In psychoanalysis it has led to a retreat into the consulting room, with an unhealthy fixation with 'pathology', more often than not defined by society, while education has become infatuated with the acquisition of culturally approved skills and, for those that can, the construction of an unblemished C.V. Both now appear to be in the business of inculcating a repertoire of 'life skills'. Education, like much of modern clinical psychotherapy, appears increasingly to centre around forms of renunciation: of simple pleasures, the indefinite postponement of present gratifications, impulse control and the suspicion of spontaneity, and an overweening preoccupation with adaptation to reality. In the process, what is being lost in both the classroom and the consulting room?

Despite this, it is my belief, which I hope is expressed in this book, that both education and psychoanalysis can reclaim their positions as philosophies of liberation, rather than forms of coercive tyranny.

Both can teach us that we are far more complex than we dare to imagine; both are in the business of creatively managing change; and both can help us rediscover informal pleasures. Psychoanalysis can help us understand the journey from learning to want to wanting to learn, and the obstacles along the way. Why do some of us want to learn while others are suspicious or defiant?

Psychotherapy and education are at best, or at least, conversations with another. In writing this book, I anxiously pondered whether I would be talking to myself, and have attempted to overcome this by a succession of dialogues with an imaginary reader. I hope this book will stimulate something similar in the reader. It is not intended to be a definitive statement about the application of psychoanalytic insights into the field of education, merely an attempt to address the issue of whether in education we are asking ourselves the right questions. As students we are constantly being told to read the question carefully; I hope this book will help us think about whether we are attempting to answer the real questions.

Introduction

None of the applications of psychoanalysis has excited so much interest and aroused so many hopes . . . as its use in the theory and practice of education . . . [psychoanalysis] has shown how the child lives on, almost unchanged, in the sick man as well as in the dreamer and the artist; it has thrown light on the motive forces and impulses, which set its characteristic stamp upon the childish nature and it has traced the stages through which a child grows up to maturing. It is not surprising therefore that an expectation should have arisen that [psychoanalysis] would benefit the work of education, whose aim it is to guide and assist children upon that forward path and to shield them from going astray (Sigmund Freud, 1936).

Psychoanalysis suggests that it is rarely clear whether psychological symptoms are problems, or attempted cures and imagined solutions. So it is with education. What is it for and how do we know when it has failed or succeeded? We are never quite sure what education is meant to teach us or what we want to learn. Is it something we need or desire? Does education enrich or deplete us? In succeeding or failing, whose agenda are we addressing?

In this book I am attempting to question whether education is merely a matter of cognitive ability aligned with 'good-enough' teaching. Just as psychoanalysis is becoming more concerned with meaning rather than explanation, I shall be reflecting on what it means to study. Learning may not be able to flourish until there is some 'acknowledgement of the subjective meaning of the curriculum for the students'. In a graphic and moving example of this, Jones (1968) recounts the experience of showing a group of students a film about an Eskimo's family leaving an older family member on the ice pack to die. When asked to reflect on the film, few were able to do so – or creatively learn from it – since many were living with elderly relatives at the time, and became paralyzed by a preoccupation with their own families.

Our attitude to education is influenced by what it represents to us. We are frequently encouraged to believe that intellect and emotions are two mutually contradictory aspects of education; the former leading to mastery, the latter to misery or failure. The function of this split is to deny the importance of affective education; this, despite the fact that emotional (and nutritional) metaphors are often used in describing the process of learning (Wittenberg, 1983; Meltzer, 1973). To learn we might need to make the experience of learning ours; something that makes sense in our personal narrative. Otherwise it is in danger of becoming a demand which invites either a spurious compliance or rebellious subversion. It is the difference between doing something for the other in expectation of a real or imagined reward, and doing something of value for oneself.

Freud defined mental health as the ability to love and to work; in education we may have to love our work, or at least invest it with something of personal value. In Chapter 1 I shall be exploring how difficult that may be during adolescence. In Chapter 2 I develop the idea of study as a metaphor for developmental transitions. Becoming a student ensures that education, if not learning, is inherently fused with our hopes and fears about our own development – that is, our personal scripts. If that is so, then these may influence how we seek to use, or abuse, others.

Given that study happens in a context, Chapter 3 explores the frequently held belief that learning is a solely cerebral activity, and is something we can do on our own, or to ourselves. Can true learning occur outside a relationship? In looking at developmental theory and what implications it may have for the process of learning and thinking, of particular relevance is the move from an individual or one-person focused psychology to a theory which stresses the interactional nature of development. Can theory help us to understand why thinking, as opposed to having thoughts, is so difficult? Why is the ability to remain curious so problematic? Do we need others in order to think and evoke our curiosity? What are the obstacles to reflective thought? If we are ambivalent about our need for others, do we harbour a fundamental ambivalence towards the spirit of enquiry? If we need others to develop, does an aesthetic of mothering, or parenting, lead us to expect the same from education?

To expand and explore the notion of a subjective project in education, Chapter 4 discusses the possibility that education can be an attempt to metamorphose the self. Why should we want to become someone, or something, different? Education may help or hinder us in this transformation, and if so, what are the implications for ourselves and our teachers? While the undergraduate student may have some, if only rudimentary, version of themselves which they aspire to become during the course of their studies, education as a process which can lead to a personal transformation will be more critical at other stages of student life. It is in this context that both graduate and mature students are discussed. I have also included in this chapter some thoughts on student suicide and self-harm. There has in recent years been increasing concern about such issues in higher education, with many reasons suggested as to why students are a particularly vulnerable group. My reason for including this issue in this chapter is my belief that in order to understand as well as help the suicidal student we may need to seek out and acknowledge a transformational script behind the thoughts of self-harm.

Chapter 5 arose out of my experience of treating an increasing number of overseas students in the context of a student medical centre. What became undeniable in more and more consultations was the number of overseas students, often from specific areas of the world, who presented with physical ailments despite repeated medical investigations having revealed no organic cause. It led me to the belief that these students were communicating something with their bodies, and, since many of the students came from cultures where unhappiness or unease is given a different meaning (and frequently where the notion of individual psychological explanations for mental states is absent), to speculate on what may happen if we do not have a method for converting certain emotional states or experiences into the realm of the psychological. Can we speak with our bodies, and what is it that is being communicated? Given the increasing economic necessity of 'recruiting' overseas students, we may need to be taught something about the cultures from which they have come. The desire to and the process of becoming an overseas student may also mask a transformational wish.

Chapter 6 addresses the issue of gender in higher education, more specifically, the debate on female under-functioning, for which a number of hypotheses have been advanced. My intention is to approach the topic from a more explicitly psychodynamic perspective, and use developmental theory and the concept of the internal saboteur to reflect on how certain traits become identified with gender and then incorporated into the educational system. The ease with which we slip into bipolar models (intellect vs emotions, reason vs intuition, hard vs soft subjects) which reinforce psychic splits may function to reinforce gender differences in education. Additionally, in this chapter I reflect on the widespread unease felt towards 'clever girls'; a discomfort many intelligent and able women share.

A recent discussion on a network news programme where students and educational institutions were encouraged to 'aggressively market themselves' was the starting point for Chapter 7. What happens to education and its students when they are encouraged to become commodities? Since learning takes place in a context, the context might define what we need to do to become 'educated'. This is as true of educational institutions, which can promote certain forms of learning at the expense of others, as of the wider society. If society defines what education is, and what it is for, then we will learn from society what we need to do to 'become educated'. In a culture dominated by the language of the market, education's function may be to help us become marketable. What is the cost? Learning and thinking may only have functional relevance – what is in it for us? – and we may grasp at what are termed 'narcissistic solutions'.

Chapter 8 is an attempt to explore our ambivalence about the concept of cleverness. Why is it admired and denigrated in about equal measure? What is being clever meant to solve? Why has cleverness – as opposed to intelligence – got such a bad press? Has psychoanalysis reinforced the split between intellect and the emotions to the extent that we assume people have to choose one or the other? Is it inevitable that being clever implies we are out of touch with our emotions? Equally, does being clever mean we will effortlessly sail through our examinations? The topic of examinations leads on to a discussion of whether the notion of 'the test' is deeply embodied in our psyches, and speaks to some profound existential angst which links back to earlier issues of development and transition.

If, as will be suggested, education and acquiring qualifications is like a playground for developmental conflicts to be addressed and worked through, then the question we need to ask ourselves is: why do we want to become qualified, and what do we want to become qualified for? It is unfortunate that this question is posed at a time in our lives when we are least equipped to answer it.

1
Adolescence

The demand to be educated during adolescence confronts us with what appears to be a paradox: at a time of life when we most want to forget, act impulsively, or avoid reflection, we most need to remember, comply, and perform. We accept that adolescence is a period of rebelliousness, confusion, and upheaval; yet at the same time expect our adolescents to engage in what we term 'formal education', which makes demands on them that, as we shall see, are difficult to meet.

We want to ablate our adolescence; adolescence is a period we viscerally experience and subsequently do our utmost to forget. As adults it is all too easy to forget our adolescent selves; through a process of selective amnesia we retain events or incidents, but at the expense of recapturing the emotional states of turmoil and inertia which pervaded those years:

> . . . memories contain no more than the bare facts . . . What we fail to recover as a rule is the atmosphere in which the adolescent lives, his anxieties, the height of elation, the depth of despair, the quickly rising enthusiasms, the utter hopelessness, the burning – at other times sterile – intellectual and philosophical preoccupations, the yearning for freedom, the sense of loneliness, the feelings of oppression by parents, the impotent rages or active hates directed against the adult world, the erotic crushes, the suicidal phantasies. These elusive mood swings are difficult to revive (Freud, A., 1958).

This clearly poses problems, not merely for those with parental, pedagogic, or pastoral responsibilities for young people, but also for those who write about adolescence as a developmental stage. It may well be that it is only through the recreation of our own experience of adolescence that we can begin to understand the dilemmas of today's adolescents as they manifest themselves in education.

In this chapter I shall be addressing the paradox that at a time in our lives when we most want to forget, or act impulsively without reflection, a demand is made to remember and become educated. How has this come about? Who had decided this?

I shall approach this conundrum by examining the concept of adolescence in relation to individual development, the influence of families, peers, and culture, highlighting the implications for education. The question is raised whether education is a conspiracy to master or tame our adolescent selves. What is the function of education in adolescent development, and how congruent is it with psychological development? Part of the problem in writing about adolescence is that psychoanalytic attempts to do so tend to produce generalizations about people, while adolescents themselves are trying to be both as unique and different as possible, as well as seeking succour in 'sameness'. In this sense this book faces exactly the same problem in relation to psychoanalytic theory as the adolescent does in life: endeavouring to synthesize similarities and differences in an attempt to be uniquely different, yet reassuringly similar.

It may be noted that 'we' is often used in describing specific experiences and affective states. It may well be asked: who are 'we' talking about? Is this book assuming a 'we' that does not exist? This corresponds to the adolescent's desire and hurry to become a 'we', while simultaneously fearing the possibility of being engulfed by the collective 'we'. 'We' in this sense not only speaks to the fact that these are developmental imperatives that all of us face, but also to the adolescent desire to be both normal – a 'we' – and different – an 'I'.

Why do we need to forget? What happens during this time which prompts us to attempt to draw a veil over this period of our lives? Is adolescence a problem, and if so, for whom? Generalizations about such a diffuse period of our lives are difficult. The *Oxford English Dictionary* defines adolescence as a '. . . growing up period between childhood and maturity over a period of ten years'; but even here we may be addressing various different processes during adolescence rather than a single developmental stage. The position is further complicated by wide individual differences in the timing of the maturational process, as well as the fact that physical and emotional aspects of development do not run parallel.

What are the tasks of adolescence, and what are the obstacles to their achievement? It is interesting to speculate on who decides these tasks: how are they constructed, and whose interests do they serve? The tasks that we are asked to negotiate, if not resolve, at this time include: identity formation (the establishment of a coherent sense of self); emotional and physical differentiation from one's family (often coinciding with a physical separation associated with education); establishing satisfactory peer relationships; accommodation to one's sexual maturation inherent in one's rapidly changing body; an often premature need to make some vocational decision; and the establishment of some ethical and philosophical view of life which may or may not be very different from one's parents'. We may wish or hope to achieve these tasks while, if experienced as too threatening or problematic, simultaneously attempt to avoid them. In some sense these tasks are our anatomical, cultural, and socially prescribed destiny; we cannot avoid being influenced by them, but equally we need to acknowledge that these are tasks ascribed to us over which we have little control; we, of course, may have our own secretly coveted projects which may or may not be congruent with those externally demanded of us.

Latency and early adolescence

The move from the family via the school into the world is facilitated by acquiring new skills, or handicapped by accentuating real or imagined deficits. Education will in part determine our competence in relation to these new skills, and one's ability to successfully negotiate this prior to adolescence will to some extent determine how we enter puberty and adolesence proper. During latency or middle childhood, major educational and developmental transitions have to be negotiated. Learning shifts from being an intra-familial experience to becoming more social; the child will be beginning to compare and contrast his two environments; home and school, parent and teacher. New opportunities arise for the displacement and reworking of familial relationships, both with peers and with teachers.

Early adolescence is ushered in by the undeniable physical changes which mark the end of latency. While latency is seen as the stage where there is a relative moratorium in psychosexual curiosity, in early adolescence one's psychosexual development becomes a primary source of interest as a result of the physical changes of puberty. One is immediately confronted with those issues we thought we had left behind between the ages of four and six: sexual curiosity, rivalry, and competition. These may have lain dormant or merely hibernated during latency; puberty ushers in a form of psychic spring, with its hopes and fears of what is to come.

An early indication that latency is drawing to a close and adolescence is approaching is often given by clear behavioural signs: lack of concentration, mood swings, a more ambivalent attitude to authority, and the beginnings of increasing attempts to conform to peer-group values. It is a curious coincidence that this happens just at the point at which the child enters secondary education with all its attendant pressures and demands.

Second infancy

While latency may invite us to become more social and outgoing, early- to mid-adolescence begins a process of self-preoccupation, often in relation to one's changing body and the increasing realization, if not altogether pleasant, of one's separateness from others.

Psychoanalytic theory suggests that while the early stage of adolescence can be seen to pick up issues from the Oedipal stage of development (negotiating triangles in the service of physical and psychological development), mid-adolescence, with the crucial issues of autonomy and independence, can be seen to link with the anal, second infantile stage, with its preoccupation with control and autonomy, shame, and pride. Late adolescence, in its concern with the 'self-in-the-world' (issues of purpose, vocation, and identity) can be seen to re-arouse our primary anxieties and preoccupations as babies of establishing a rudimentary sense of self and trust in a benign rather than malign environment. Adolescence then forces us to confront and rework earlier stages of development, seemingly in reverse order. Freud (1905) suggested that '... the individual recapitulates and expands in the second decennium of life the development he passed through during the first five years'.

If adolescence is a repetition, what is it that we repeat, and are we condemned to experience the same outcome? Ernest Jones' (1948) 'general law' of adolescence may well be excessively deterministic:

> ... adolescence recapitulates infancy and ... the precise way in which a given person will pass through the necessary stages of development in adolescence is to a very great extent determined by the form of his infantile development ... these stages are passed through on different places at the two periods of infancy and adolescence, but in very similar ways in the same individual.

It does allow, however, for the possibility that adolescence offers an opportunity to make sense of infancy as well as to rework or revise it. It provides us with a second chance, or window of opportunity, to deal with issues that may have been problematic or problematically gratifying at earlier stages of development.

If indeed, as psychoanalysis would suggest, adolescence is a recapitulation of our infantile lives, we have to ask whether adolescents are toddler *manqués*? If so, what distinguishes the two stages? In infancy we are occupied with oral gratifications or frustrations, and issues of weaning and trust in others are paramount. Following on from this, issues of control, autonomy, shame, and disgust dominate the anal stage while infancy is brought to a close through the resolution or otherwise of the Oedipal dilemma. Does the attraction to the parent of the opposite sex inevitably mean killing off the same-sex parent, or does one have to relinquish incestuous wishes as a result, partly of prohibitions (and fear of retaliation) and partly through the dawning awareness of one's physical limitations? This involves the recognition of a triangular relationship from which, in important aspects, one is excluded. Disappointment, yet safety ushers in the period of calm during latency, although not without a rudimentary sense of guilt in relation to one's incestuous desires and murderous phantasies. We need to relinquish some desires in the service of psychic and external reality; not, however, without some unease, guilt and a reluctant compliance being two possible outcomes. In infancy we need to negotiate a physical separateness from (m)others during the first three years of our lives. This 'first individuation process' is facilitated through a form of internalization, that is, the recognition that there is a mother 'out' there, but there is also a good image of a mother inside oneself, which keeps us going when our mothers are not there. (We need, of necessity, to return to base from time to time for refuelling.) This physical weaning leads to a recognition of separateness and the ability to distinguish between what is me and what is the other.

Individuation

In this sense adolescence can be viewed, as Bloss (1962) calls it, a 'second individuation process'. The psychological dilemma which confronts us is similar to the one we faced in infancy; the consequences of the physiological and physical changes of puberty lead to an intensification or reawakening of our physical and psychological desires of loving and hating, but this time in the context of a physically mature body. What we have formerly been physically incapable of becomes within the realm of possibility. Former prohibitions come to be seen as potentially illusory; anything is possible. The adolescent is faced with the same conundrum as the infant and toddler; the strong intensification of physiological energies confronting a precarious or brittle sense of identity. Awakening sexuality, however, pushes the adolescent to look outside the immediate family for objects of desire or love which challenge the emotional ties with the parents.

Infancy and adolescence have certain things in common, including the demand on the individual to adapt to maturation and increasing autonomy. In adolescence it is not merely a process of physical weaning or severance, although indeed it often involves this as the adolescent moves into higher education, as it was during the first individuation process. The second transition involves an emotional weaning; not just from the physical prescence of our parents but also from those subjective parents which we built up in our minds. In adolescence these 'subjective parents' may or may not bear any resemblance to our real or objective parents. The creation of the internal tyrant is perhaps an important developmental achievement. It is not uncommon to hear an adolescent rail furiously against the oppressive unreasonableness of their parents or teachers, only subsequently to meet the parent who is eminently reasonable, concerned and sensitive to their adolescent child's needs; the circle is squared by accepting the subjective truth – the adolescent's need to create an ogre (possibly through the projection of uncomfortable aggressive and persecutory feelings) in their minds as something to rebel against in their attempts to gradually disengage from the parent in the quest for autonomy and independence. Individuation requires the severance of childhood emotional attachments, but to successfully complete that we may need to go back and relive them. In this sense we may need to repeat earlier stages of development, which carries with it the danger of using this repetition defensively, i.e. to retreat and avoid any progression.

Adolescence, then, involves the gradual disengagement from the family and the psychological adaptation to the physically maturing body. Secrets and fantasies which were safe in a pre-pubertal body now have to be repeated and reviewed in the context of an increasingly mature body. Our bodies change shape and size, uncontrollably evoking excitement and fear in equal measure. Freud believed one's own body, and one's initial relationship to it via the mother, to be the fundamental foundation of future psychic structure. A relationship to or with one's own body therefore precedes a sense of self. Our physical self and our relationship to it assumes a central preoccupation throughout our lives; even though the meaning we attach to it may well change from one developmental period to the next. During adolescence, increasing sexual maturity and the ability to procreate add a new dimension to both one's previous relationship to one's body and to our psychological capacity to incorporate this quantum leap – it is as though the technology has outstripped an emotional capacity to master it.

Physical change

Among the physical changes are ones that irrefutably confirm our genders. These can no longer be denied, and attempts to do so, which may well have been possible during one's childhood, will inevitably lead the adolescent into difficulties. Growth and development seemingly become arbitrary and do not proceed logically. Preoccupations about normality – and the physical changes, or lack of them – become commonplace.

I was once consulted by a tall, miserable, physically impressive 16-year-old boy, who was sent by his form master, who was concerned that the boy looked miserable for no apparent reason. After four meetings, he told me his secret; he did not have any hair on his chest, which he found both humiliating and shameful, fearing he was odd, different and in some way deficient. It became apparent that this anxiety was extensively handicapping in his life; he refused to go swimming or do P.E. without wearing a vest, much to the consternation, bewilderment, and frustration of his teachers. He was so embarrassed by this that he refused to take his clothes off while on a summer beach holiday with his parents. Seeing his sporty, athletic, and 'hairy' father merely added to his misery, and confirmed his feelings of worthlessness and inadequacy. He eventually was able to talk about his feelings of general inadequacy and doubts about his competence and acceptability over a wide range of areas. His symptom had acted as a metaphor which needed decoding.

The concept of the 'growth spurt' in adolescence is a curious one; certainly our bodies change almost overnight, but equally many adolescents wonder when that mysterious physical attribute is going, if ever, to appear. Central to this is the issue of identity, i.e. who one is in relation to oneself and the world. Identity implies some form of consistency, which is challenged and undermined if one's body and appearance are notoriously inconsistent, chameleon-like, and uncontrollable. The body's function also changes; from being previously something that gratifies or frustrates oneself, it now has in addition the capacity to gratify or frustrate others. Sex, and reciprocal sexual encounters, are now reality, rather than as previously safely existing in a sexually immature body.

These physical changes clearly have psychological consequences. Just as we are asked to face a number of generic tasks in adolescence, our changing bodies make rather more specific demands on us. Accepting an adult role challenges the adolescent to accept the new sexual body, which is either male or female but can't be both; although, clearly, in fantasy any number of permutations may exist. In fantasy we may wish or fear to be both or neither. One is faced with other sexual bodies, different from one's own, a difference which confirms our own limitations; in this sense anatomy becomes destiny which can only be changed or modified in fantasy.

Our bodies then become central preoccupations during adolescence, inviting us to adapt to questions of control, adequacy, sexual orientation, and mutuality in relationships. This, together with the issues of separation and individuation, invites us to take responsibility for our bodies and ourselves. We may decline the invitation, of course, but at some cost.

Many adolescents experience their bodies as enemies over which they have no control. Changing adolescent bodies can come to symbolize certain forms of conflict and act as metaphors for, among other things, whether we want to grow up or not, relationships with others (especially peers and parents), and how comfortable we feel with our emerging selves. As a consequence the frequently seen attacks against the self in adolescence (self-injury, mutilation, eating problems, recklessness, and the almost determined desire to put oneself in potentially dangerous situations), assume a symbolic significance; they become not only attacks against the self, but also against a subjectively experienced persecutor (an example would be the stranglehold of the parents in one's mind):

A 21-year-old woman in the second year of her undergraduate degree consulted me feeling uneasy, but unclear what the source of that unease could be. She had been to a prestigious school and achieved two As and a B at A-level. She was a charming, attractive, and sophisticated young woman who was 'terribly good company'. I learnt she was an only child of a wealthy family.

She eventually told me, with a great deal of shame, humiliation and self-reproach, that she was floridly bulimic and had been throughout her adolescence; she would eat biscuits, cakes, ice-creams, after which she would rush to the toilet and vomit. When this didn't work she made extensive use of laxatives, then for days she would eat just oranges. Effectively both food and her body were out of control. It became apparent after a number of meetings that this uncomfortable, suspicious attitude to food extended to other possible gratifications; with men she would oscillate between avoiding them and being wildly promiscuous; in her academic work she would sit in tutorials without saying a word, feeling triumphant, but subsequently feeling contemptuous with herself for withholding and not eagerly partaking of what intellectual food was on offer. Feeling empty and cleansed, was preferable to feeling full and gross.

She eventually talked about hating her body and femininity, which she felt she had to control. Perhaps she could stop her own emerging sexuality and physical development? She had a comforting fantasy where she visualized herself as a comely, plump, middle-aged mother of three, a gratifying scene, which implied that she could somehow avoid the turbulence of adolescence, young adulthood, and sexuality, which she experienced as frightening and confusing. If only she could skip a couple of generations overnight and avoid the messy bits. The difficulty, however, was that this meant immediately turning into her mother. This was a yearning for those halcyon days of pre-pubertal bliss, when relationships with boys and bodies were rather more straightforward. Perhaps controlling her body via food could be a way in which she was vainly attempting to cling on to being different from her mother, a denial of physical reality; she desperately wanted to be different from her mother, but maturation merely confirmed that she was becoming the same or similar. The adolescent task of differentiating herself from her mother carried with it the danger that she was destined to be the same.

Our adolescent, physically maturing bodies confirm that we deterministically have no choice but to become like, in a certain sense at least, one of our parents. Perhaps this is why we need to continually assault them? Self-mutilation or self-starvation, recklessness over the use of their bodies may well coincide with some ambivalence over whether they want to become like the same-sex parent, while also coinciding with a subjective experience of their bodies as unsafe and dangerous. Symbolically or in fantasy, who else have we got to blame for our bodies except our parents, more particularly, mothers? The mother, who protected the childhood body, now becomes its persecutor. However, hatred of those who gave us our bodies makes us feel even worse, and the temptation is to transform it into self-contempt.

One's ambivalence and hatred of one's own body can also represent a hatred of those internal, subjective parents, who bequeathed them to us, indeed they may not be ours, merely parental gifts; to be given something one does not want, or has no need for, or has no knowledge of what to do with, is every child's nightmare. Does the maturing body belong to oneself, or is it an alien presence belonging to another: '. . . the earliest feelings of love and hatred from the parents become part of the love or hatred by the child of his own body . . . for the first time in the person's life he experiences his own body as the source or reservoir of his love or hatred containing those objects who love or hate, protect or threaten' (Laufer, 1984).

The adolescent is faced with the demand to jettison the safety of the pre-pubertal body, since attempts to remain in a child's body will inevitably lead to difficulties. This does not preclude, however, the establishment of a secret relationship to a body in fantasy, very different from one's own.

Unlike the child, the adolescent's passionate, if ambivalent, feelings of love and hate now become very real; they can be enacted. It is perhaps interesting to speculate on gender-specific problems at this age; if, as we have seen, girls are destined to develop bodies which are similar to their mothers', de-identifying from them will be a life-long task. For boys, their bodies may well be a way of separating from their mothers; developing a body similar to father may 'rescue' the male adolescent from his mother, while placing him firmly in the context of a continued rivalrous comparison with the father. At least by attacking our bodies there is something we can do to relieve ourselves of the feelings of passive paralysis, shame, and humiliation in relation to this new and disturbing creation. The body may become not merely an estranged, malign companion, but also a constant reminder of one's own abnormality, and the fact that pre-pubertal solutions to the emotional impact of our physical selves are no longer possible or appropriate. We have to take a stand in relation to our physical selves; it is not something we can deny or avoid without it becoming excessively problematic.

Separation and loss

If one of the demands in adolescence is to take ownership of one's body, however frightening this may be, the second demand is an emotional separation from those who have nurtured us in the past. Delinquency, aggression, compulsive behaviour, educational under-functioning can be seen as attempts to detach oneself from parental prohibitions and reduce the reliance on parental approbation. Separation involves loss involves mourning.

Puberty, like every other developmental milestone becomes both an achievement and a loss. The withdrawal both from our childhood parents and bodies is not achieved without considerable ambivalence, and is by definition problematic. We may struggle to tolerate two contradictory ideas in our minds: the wish to grow up and the wish to remain a child. Behaviourally and emotionally it may lead to two contradictory forces being observable; the need for disengagement and yet continuous sustenance from the parents and others such as teachers and counsellors, which leads to the ubiquitous and repetitive cycles of emotional withdrawal and return. This can be seen to be reminiscent of the toddler exploring ever-increasing distance from its mother, but continually needing to return. The return journey may often provide comfort but can be experienced as confirming one's fears of one's own deficits, limitations, and dependence, and consequently a continual reminder that we cannot survive on our own. The emotional and behavioural lability so prevalent in adolescence can be ascribed to this developmental paradox; we want to grow up and yet yearn to still be childlike. The temperamental oscillations seen in the same person between dependency and passivity on the one hand, and activity and independence on the other reflect the excitement and fear of the developmental process. Inherent in this is the demand for the separation from the internal and external parents in the search for an individuality which is uniquely different, yet safely similar.

Separation may involve becoming different or giving oneself permission to stay the same or similar:

> A 14-year-old was referred to me by his perplexed form master with an accompanying note: 'Thank you for seeing this young man, a quiet, industrious and able 14-year-old. He was found last week to have in his possession a variety of substances which we quickly identified as being chemical materials capable of producing a nasty explosion. Quite apart from being against school rules, the headmaster and I were naturally concerned that he was involved in this kind of experimentation. He is an extremely able scientist who has been interested in the spectacular aspects of chemistry for some time, experimenting with a variety of such substances for a year or so at home.'

> He was a somewhat secretive, ruminative young man for whom doing things on his own was of supreme importance; hence the fact that he refused the opportunity to continue this experimentation with others, under supervision, in class or in the context of the science club.

> He was an only child who came from a family where his father was away for long periods, and he had developed a rather uneasy closeness to his mother. He was in awe of her; she was indeed spectacular, but he also at times found her constant intrusiveness into his life, activities, and thoughts inhibiting and annoying, evoking a feeling of wanting to liberate himself from her influence, but being unable to even contemplate this. This awesome mother was eventually revealed to be the head of the chemistry department at a neighbouring school. Spectacular 'explosions' clearly now took on a different dimension; his preoccupation with his relationship with his mother could be re-enacted in science; she was a spectacular source of wonder in his life, but how tempting it would be to blow up her influence on him. In a way it reflected his adolescent despair about growing apart from her; he was faced with remaining totally identified with her (an identification which was sometimes pleasurable; he really enjoyed chemistry) as a dutiful classroom chemist, or totally removing her influence on him, metaphorically blowing her up. Only by blowing her up could he *choose* to remain similar.

Loss of parents

Adolescence prompts us to review the relationships with our parents. We may have been dimly aware during latency that there was something slightly flawed about our parents, but it is only during adolescence that we are invited to see our parents as fully three-dimensional. We need to tease out those aspects of parental identifica-tions with which we feel comfortable, from those which are less comforting. We need to be disillusioned, yet need to do it ourselves. A developmentally appropriate preoccupation with issues of similarity or difference from one's parents may lead to oscillations between grandiosity ('I am better than them') and subservience ('I am worthless and need their protection').

Grandiosity involves denigration of the other; this can involve the rejection of parental beliefs, attitudes, discipline, or lives. We have, at this point in our lives, to destroy before we can create. Part of the grandiosity is based on a profound denial; what is denied is one's own helplessness, incompetence, and loss of parental support or encour-agement. Grandiosity can involve rejecting what the pre-pubertal parents have stood for, while embracing values totally opposed to those of the parents. This denigrating grandiosity can easily switch to its polar opposite; subservient and passive dependence where the parental loss is experienced as so crippling that the only recourse is to seek and cling on to parental protection. Attitudes to learning can become a reflection of these struggles.

The childhood idealization of the parents is replaced by substitute sources of identification, be they peers, pop stars, or teachers. These aid the transition to an identity which is much more securely our own. However, losing our childhood parents is unlikely to immediately enrich us; we are left with an emptiness, a vacuum where something has been lost, but it is unclear what, if anything, has or will be gained. The parents may not physically have been lost, but what is being mourned is their childhood versions. Feelings of sadness and despair may not merely be in response to a tangible loss, but also a result of our increasing awareness of our difficulty in loving or valuing a person who has been previously loved. Not being able to feel what we ought to feel towards the people who brought us up may induce feelings of guilt and anger.

Mourning and loss may well be adaptive and aid the adolescent process; it is only through letting go what is 'lost' that we can free ourselves to find something new. In this sense, adolescent depression may well be functional; health in adolescence could be defined as having survived the inevitable teenage depression, not merely in relation to a perceived loss, but also in respect of anxieties and doubts over whether we will be able to adequately master adulthood. It may also be that one not only mourns the childhood parents but also the parents one never had; the Freudian 'family romance' – where we believed in the fantasy that we were conceived by more noble or 'superhuman' parents, and only temporarily placed with our families – must finally be renounced. We must come to terms with what we have had, rather than that which might have been. This does not prevent, indeed makes it rather more likely, that our ambivalence toward parental figures will be displaced and repeated in relation to both education and teachers/tutors.

Separation forces us to face the stark choice between withdrawal from the family into the outside world, or to forego and reject the outside world and its potential gratifications and frustrations, and attempt to cling to the family, and one's childhood self, in a form which may become problematic. Denial, via an enmeshed attachment to the parents, or flight, via impulsive actions or gestures, can be reflections of this, but both are attempts to master separation. This isolation and confusion may well be reinforced by a very tangible sensation that one has metaphorically killed off one's parents. To put it another way: in order to develop one has to supplant, if not 'murder', one's parents; small wonder that for some adolescents this has to be avoided, with a forestalling of their own development. Winnicott (1972), while being the most gentle of *agent provocateurs*, indicates that for development to proceed we may need to feel comfortable with a part of ourselves which could seriously contemplate homicide:

> If the child is to become an adult, then this move is achieved over the dead body of an adult, where there is the challenge of the growing boy or girl, there let the adult meet the challenge. And it will not necessarily be nice.

In the play of the younger child, death and destruction, while ubiquitous, is in general imaginary; for the adolescent, 'murder' becomes possible; one is symbolically invited to 'kill off' the parent by taking their place. This may influence how far we feel we have we been given or allowed ourselves permission to succeed, as opposed to needing to subvert ourselves through failure. If this is true, then it clearly has consequences for both educational under- and over-functioning.

Suicidal preoccupations and escapism have the effect of killing off the parents inside oneself as a displacement from homicidal feelings towards the actual parent. It is amusing to note that Eric Erikson (1956) recounts that in his early work with adolescents he had to be tentative in suggesting that young people might hate their parents, while later, when this idea had clearly struck a chord, he had to be equally cautious about suggesting that they might like them as well. These two seemingly polar opposites may not merely co-exist, but be facets of the same effect. The actual death of a parent during this period, not an infrequent experience during one's time as a student, can reinforce these homicidal anxieties and prevent negative feelings being acknowledged and metabolized.

Parents can stand in the way of us becoming adults and therefore condemn us to go on being children. Consequently, any authority relationship during adolescence (including student-teacher) is likely to reflect similar preoccupations. Indeed the issue is frequently much more intense for students who, by being financially dependent on their parents well into adulthood, are presented with a particularly difficult dilemma: that is, requiring very tangible parental support yet at the same time psychologically needing to rebel against them. What better way than for the struggle to be displaced and enacted with the student's subject, course, tutor or educational institution?

Ambivalence and solutions

Perhaps more than at any other stage in the life-cycle, ambivalence is the dominant state of mind during adolescence. We are no longer children, chattels of our parents, nor fully adult. We are plagued by doubts (often masked by overactivity or inertia), about our competence, adequacy, or acceptability. We can grasp at often illusory straws that fend off development or speak to our ambivalence. Inconsistencies in speech, manners, attitudes, or beliefs will reflect this ambivalence. Each of us as adolescents will need to decide whether the gains of development will outweigh the disadvantages. Where the losses are potentially too great and the advantages too demanding, we may well attempt to stand still or prevent change. If we fear growing up and all that that implies, or are given the impression by others that it is too high a hurdle, then we may self-destructively sabotage one or more areas of our lives (social, personal, educational) which potentially lead to independence.

For those for whom the loss of their childhood selves and the progression to adulthood appears too problematic, there are a number of potential, if flawed, solutions readily recognizable in educational settings. Take the ascetic adolescent who combines a peculiar form of renunciation of physical pleasures with a withdrawal into oneself to avoid or attempt to deny change. Any pursuit of pleasurable gratification, including intellectual curiosity, is viewed with suspicion, and what is seen is a withdrawn, lifeless, academically under-functioning adolescent. This can frequently involve hypochondriacal preoccupations or secretly held omnipotent phantasies from which others are excluded; reality needs to be kept at bay. Conversely, the verbose, grandiose, adolescent will intellectualize as a way of attempting to control and master physical and emotional changes, and engage the uncomprehending adult in highly intellectual, seemingly abstract, discussions on philosophical issues, the form of which may be very different from their content: seemingly cerebral discussions may reflect some deep-seated personal concerns about unfamiliar and potentially disturbing erotic or aggressive feelings. Equally, silence, or an essay withheld, may be defiance (a refusal to submit or comply), or an adolescent flight from an intra-psychic conflict: one of the advantages of silence or negation for an adolescent may well be that it symbolically represents a magical fusion with a person from the past; a refusal to communicate during adolescence may well represent a way we maintain contact with our pre-pubertal lives and our pre-pubertal relationships with our parents.

The need for control

A further way in which we may seek to exert some control over what is experienced as uncontrollable is to act outwardly in an attempt to negate our own passivity and helplessness in relation to our adolescent selves. Delinquency, promiscuity, drug or alcohol abuse may be the most striking manifestations of this process, and the world of education is frequently the forum for this dilemma to be addressed:

Charles, a 17 year old, was on the point of expulsion. Bright but feckless, with huge potential but with an equally large capacity for undermining himself, he was sent to me by his headmaster. He was not working, drinking to excess, drugs were suspected, and he was insolent, showed no remorse, and was generally a problem. He presented to me as described: cocky, dismissive, taking great pride in his alcohol consumption, and contemptuous of those adults around him who he roughly divided into those that were genuinely concerned for him (who were experienced as weak, indulgent and pathetic), and those who were firm, strict, who earned his respect, but were just there to be outwitted and undermined – a challenge Charles accepted with great ease and gusto.

His behaviour had brought him huge popularity among his peers, which was of extreme importance to him. He reluctantly came to see me (it gave him an excuse to miss double maths), full of bravado, and I despaired of being able to get any leverage on the problem.

At our fourth meeting he let slip that on his last pub crawl he had walked past the dole office and the words 'That's the life' came to his mind. I showed some interest in this; it was a relief from the unrelenting bravado with which he communicated with me, and he relaxed somewhat and went on to talk about a life with no responsibilities. When we took this to its logical conclusion, in his mind he thought he would like to be a dustman; no teachers, parents, counsellors urging him to do well and comply; merely a community of dustpersons, of equals, no pressure; he would not have to think or worry about whether he was going to be successful. The following week when I reminded him of his dustman daydream, he told me he came from an extremely achievement-oriented, successful family and was not sure of being successful; not being sure whether 'he had it in him or not'. The drunken, insolent, indifferent youth now appeared in a very different light. When I asked him what he thought his chances of being successful were, he replied, 'No better than 50–50, which for a gambler like myself aren't great odds.' Far better for him not to even contemplate competing. Those like his father, who were successful competitors in the adult world, evoked feelings of anxiety, envy, and repulsion. Feeling ill-equipped to compete with these adult demands, Charles would undermine and mock them; drinking, drugs, cheek, took away the feelings of inadequacy.

Our helplessness demands that we negate or deny it by turning it into its opposite, yet within our adolescent confusion may be the seeds of future creativity. The wish to attain adulthood, however that is subjectively defined, while still wanting to be a child, brings into focus the anxiety that the former will lead to the jettisoning of that part of the childhood self which is imaginative and curious and able to lose oneself in exploration and play. This is not merely essential to childhood, but also to learning and creativity. Taking responsibility and authority over oneself and one's relationships, which can be perceived as frightening, needs somehow to incorporate childhood exploratory curiosity. Charles was able and bright but could not allow himself to get in touch with or value that part of himself as the fear of not living up to the expectations it provoked was overwhelming.

What may appear possible solutions at this stage become in essence developmental foreclosures; the child who truants and leaves school, or the adolescent who drops out of higher or further education could be seen as attempting to get their retaliation in first; they will inevitably be left and abandoned by education to fend for themselves, so renouncing education may well be turning a passive fear of rejection into a form of active mastery in rejecting education.

Cognitive changes

Clearly, increasing cognitive and perceptual changes during adolescence add to the complexity of the adolescent experience. A full description of cognitive changes during this period is beyond the scope of this book, but it is perhaps worth noting that puberty ushers in both a qualitative as well as a quantitative change in cognitive and intellectual function. Here again, as in so many other spheres of adolescent development, our increasing intellectual and perceptual sophistication demands some form of adaptation and mastery; the alternative is to be overwhelmed or to take refuge in cognitive over-compensation. With the advent of formal, as opposed to concrete, operational thought at puberty (Inhelder and Piaget, 1958), the adolescent becomes capable of new and increasingly subtle ways of thinking about and experiencing the world. Abstract thought becomes possible, and with it the use of metaphors and symbols; no longer are we tied to logic; abstractions can become absorbing.

This brings with it the possibility of teasing out the disparity between what is actual and what is possible, with the actual frequently found wanting or inferior. The awareness of this discrepancy between what is and what may be aids the process of reviewing the immediate past, and thinking about what should be or have been. The adolescent can become an idealist (or indeed the obverse, a nihilist) and become future oriented. While pre-pubertal life was concerned with learning how to function in the here and now, the adolescent is able much more readily to grasp not only the immediate state of things, but also the possible state they might or could assume.

An increase in the ability to generate and explore hypotheses which depart from immediately observable events, together with a heightened perceptual awareness, increases both the sensation of being involved with something greater than oneself, as well as paradoxically aiding increasing introspection and egocentricity. This can take the form of an increasing concern about ourselves, which is implicitly assumed to be shared by others. The move from logical and concrete thought, as with other aspects of adolescent development, is potentially a mixed blessing. To the order and stasis of pre-pubertal cognitive thought is now added the possibility of being truly imaginative. Whether we wish to be imaginative, or can allow ourselves to be constructively creative, can, as we shall see, become an area of considerable conflict.

The role of our peers

As we become more aware of ourselves in and of the world, our post-latency recognition of others becomes intensified. If the younger child's interest in another has been a mixture of curiosity, pleasure, and frustration, the adolescent now comes to see contemporaries as having a none-too-conscious functionality. Peers can offer us another world, or the hope of transition into it, while at the same time offering us what appears to be at the time a viable alternative. Peers present us with the possibility of an alternative way of being; if we need to find some way of freeing ourselves from the internal and external parental prohibitions of childhood, then other people, with other lives, values, and behaviours, can facilitate that transition. Psychologically, peers are used ruthlessly to experiment with being something else, or to put us in touch with a side of ourselves which courts parental disapproval. Intense yet brittle friendships offer an interim culture away from parental intrusion, and offer us a chance to experiment with something totally 'other'. Experimentation with other ways of being is on offer from the peer group, which not infrequently merely replaces one perceived tyranny with another, less clearly acknowledged or acknowledgeable, as a form of control.

If we need to leave the caretakers of our childhood, the loss becomes more bearable if we can put something in their place; something often means anything. Separation is aided by having somewhere to go; how problematic it is to loiter without intent. Love objects and sources of nurture need to be found outside the family, involving a partial renunciation of dependency, which means giving up the past, while viewing with suspicion, yet yearning for, any new relationship which potentially offers similar gratifications or frustrations. Idealization, which can be seen as a determined and specific way of not getting to know someone and avoiding intimacy and dependence, is embraced in the adolescent's desperation to be at once separate yet merged: if we are at one with a group which beatifies someone or something, then we can lose our own identity, and ambivalence about intimacy, and become totally merged or enmeshed with another. We can become something which denies asking ourselves whether we are someone. The adolescent is then re-enacting something from much earlier; unthinking fusion with the mother which functions as avoiding painful feelings about separation. Merely being with others, however, does not solve the problem of being alone. An over-valuation of intellectual and educational achievement, as well as its disavowal, can have a similar function.

Peers offer an opportunity for experimentation; same- and opposite-sex relationships offer prototypes for later adult relationships. Intense single-sex relationships would appear to offer confirmation of an identity as yet insubstantial, although carrying with it the danger of denying change through the avoidance of the opposite sex. The opposite sex is a constant reminder of difference, one's own changing appearance and its exciting yet frightening consequences. Intimacy, in an adolescent still confused about ambivalent feelings in relation to his parents, brings with it problematic issues of trust and betrayal, while forms of rebellion can be pathways to discovering new values, attitudes, and feelings. This can be in evidence and replicated in any teaching relationships.

Attachments are made only to be swiftly broken, as they are based on a particularly blinkered idealization, which can be seen as a way in which the adolescent displaces aspects of his or her own narcissism; peers or partners are frequently related to as disavowed parts of oneself. Parts of oneself can be placed into another or the group, which are then seen as external to the self, yet one's own proximity to the group enables one to control the intensity of one's experience of that particular part. The stupid one can place and renounce his cleverness in the group and vice versa. An interesting facet of this is bullying or scapegoating. Membership of a strong, powerful, invulnerable group conveys those attributes upon its membrs, leaving those excluded to represent the obverse: generally weakness and vulnerability, which the group can then persecute in the outsider. Apart from being able to disavow parts of themselves with which they may be uncomfortable, group members can then take comfort from being 'normal', 'acceptable', 'the same', as their peers and thus satisfy major adolescent preoccupations. It also conveys an, albeit externally prescribed, sense of identity.

Classrooms and tutorial groupings are settings where these problems can naturally occur, which can lead the bewildered tutor into difficulty. These settings can be viewed as a transitional space for the adolescent's need to modulate his environment *vis-à-vis* both the adult world and their peers (Meltzer, 1973)

For the post-pubertal young person peers provide relief and an alternative to the frightening closeness of dependent and intimate one-to-one relationships; this facilitates separation, yet separating from something and being able to let go presupposes that someone is open to the possibility of letting you go.

Family responses

Adolescence does not exist in a vacuum, and is stressful for reasons other than solely individual psychology; other issues will have a decisive influence on whether we move forwards, backwards, or are condemned to an uncomfortable form of stasis. Families for instance: the quest for independence and developing sexuality will evoke strong counter-responses from either parents or siblings, a response which may not always be helpful. The adolescent's ambivalence about whether he wishes to grow up is shared by the family. The family will regard every developmental step made by their child in the same way that the child experiences it: a milestone, with pleasure at its achievement as well as a loss which has to be mourned. Parents may consciously or otherwise be very reluctant to allow their children to grow up, since something of value may well be lost in their increasing independence and autonomy. This is increasingly so if the child has come to represent a displaced infantile need or gratification for the parent; if we need someone to be dependent on us to reinforce our own sense of being needed and loved, we are not going to take kindly to our offspring seeking to be both separate and more grown up than ourselves.

The reciprocal but unacknowledged mourning between parent and child is perhaps the most problematic issue for families of adolescent children to negotiate. However, just as adolescence allows the young person to rework something from the past, this opportunity is also possible for the parents, for they are forced to take a stand *vis-à-vis* their offspring, and compare their own adolescence and education with that of their child, not always comfortably, and frequently involving envy, which is masked by denigration or mockery. They are confronted as an adult couple, if not a family, by potentially uncomfortable or unresolved questions which have been shelved in the process of having a family. Adolescent despair is matched by parental confusion, but both hold the promise of being developmentally creative, since both occur during potentially difficult life-cycle transitions.

Counter-separation attitudes in parents at this stage may well be motivated and prompted by their own anxieties, making their adolescent offspring into something which must be 'managed'. Envy, jealousy, and resentment of the assumed freedoms available to their contemporary offspring can lead to the temptation of attempting to live vicariously through the young person. Examples would include severe prohibitions resultant from often unconscious envy, or too lax and indulgent parenting out of a sense of identification with their adolescent child; the parent may well take some form of pleasurable gratification from the adolescent behaving in a way which was not possible for themselves.

Parental discomfort at this may well be internalized by the adolescent himself: mutual distrust, denigration, and contempt masking loving and warm feelings. Both adolescent and parent may be forced into taking polarized positions, yearning for some conciliation, even if it must be undermined if and when it is attempted. Feelings become almost magically transformed into the opposite, one masking the other: love becomes hate, dependence turns into revolt; respect and admiration into derision and contempt. Both parties are seemingly condemned to taking positions which frequently resemble compulsions; we can be as dependent in rebellion as we are in submission. Rebellious and disapproved behaviours are tempting as they address two seemingly contradictory issues at once: differentiating from the parents as well as maintaining an often passionate and intense link with them.

Adolescent behaviour may meet with a vicarious and secret parental approval as it may be enacting something that the parents may have regretfully denied themselves during their own adolescence. Rules are made in order that attempts can be made to subvert, if not break them. Sometimes we might need someone else to challenge the system or establishment that timidity has prevented us from challenging ourselves. Tutors may not be immune from unconsciously using their students in this way. In this sense, adolescence and adolescent rebellion present adults with their repressed doubts about themselves.

Confrontation and growth

The adolescent's virulent hostility or sullen resentfulness reflects an actual passionate involvement and engagement with the parents, which is manifestly and behaviourally denied. As we have seen, these disturbing feelings can be placed into the other: aggressive feelings projected into the parents making them persecutors, while envious and rivalrous feelings can go from adult to young person, turning the adolescent into something which must be got the better of and mastered. In these circumstances the adolescent may have no recourse other than to grasp, eagerly if disappointedly, what Erikson (1968) has termed 'negative identity'. We embrace all those things we have been warned about.

For both parent and adolescent, rebellion and confrontation become developmental necessities which, paradoxically if avoided, risk impeding the developmental process of both parties. There is a certain inevitability about confrontation which plants it firmly in the context of normative adolescent development. The difficulty is that it may well be fuelled by fantasies on both sides which threaten, if not addressed or contained, to spiral out of control. The adolescent, as we have seen previously, may well feel that rebellion, if not responded to, will result in a form of psychic murder, while the parents (or tutor) may well fear the consequences, appeasement or triumph, resulting from any possible confrontation. However turbulent, these confrontations help to consolidate the adolescent's inner resources, and are in essence, although hardly recognizable, the teenage equivalent of the younger child's play.

Survival of the object

Winnicott, when talking about adolescence, stressed the importance of the parent, and by definition the teacher, surviving the relentless onslaught from their offspring (as though surviving the attempted destruction is a necessary prerequisite for creativity), whether it be active rebellion or passive withdrawal, without relinquishing any important principle. Rebelling against something is infinitely safer than rebelling against nothing. The adolescent who feels that the adult offers no resistance, capitulates, and continuously appeases, will rightly become contemptuous of the adult world and terrified of his own power and omnipotence. An adult abdication would be a Pyrrhic victory for the adolescent when what was needed was a good fight, for only then will rebellion and spontaneity feel safe. Adult abdication leaves both parties dissatisfied. The knowledge that adults care enough to stand firm and enforce suitably flexible rules enables the adolescent to feel that he has not been abandoned to his own impulses, which, as we have seen, can be frightening:

> A young man progressively came late to our meetings – first 5, then 10, then eventually 15 minutes. I was concerned at this but also aware (this was a highly impulsive and aggressive student) of a feeling in myself that I did not want to provoke a heated exchange that might lead to either aggression on his part or his ending treatment. I eventually plucked up courage to take this up with him; he was surprised, somewhat shaken, but relieved. He responded by saying he thought I had not noticed his increasing lateness (witness his increasing attempts to provoke me by coming even later), and thought it implied that I did not mind whether he came late or not: he could do as he pleased. This was both a rather uncomfortable feeling for him as well as an implication that I did not care; I did not value him or what he had to say enough to be concerned about whether he came on time or not.

A similar dynamic may be apparent in attendance at both lectures and tutorials. There is also something safe and comforting about the possibility of rebelling in the knowledge that the rebellion is being both noticed and contained. An environment or person which can allow rebellion is potentially more benign than one which insists on banishing even the idea of difference or conflict. For Winnicott, health in adolescence is having the capacity to think of oneself, and at times be thought of, as immature; the freedom to have ideas is in danger of being foreclosed by adult capitulation or total negation. Creativity and experimentation need to be free of compliance and precocious maturity. This has important implications for a university education, which needs to encourage experimentation while at the same time offering the structures which make such creative play both possible and safe. Getting it wrong may be an important process on the way to getting it right. When Winnicott originally developed his paper on adolescence, the final words of the sentence quoted earlier were '. . . but it will be fun.' Not wholly unsurprisingly, these words were omitted from the published text. We can never be sure that being in the presence of an adolescent, as parent or teacher, will be fun.

Ambivalence may result not only in a sense of wariness, anxiety about dependency and commitment, and a temptation to disassociate oneself from one's concerns, but also suggest that mutual communication may be problematic for both the adolescent and the adult. We as adolescents have left the childhood world of play, yet not fully entered the adult world of words; or even if we have, we do not know (or cannot say) what we want to say or how to say it. We may well despise that part of ourself which is vulnerable, weak, confused, and in constant need of positive approval. We may deal with our own helplessness and vulnerability by over-compensating in the opposite direction; we become or identify with versions of self-sufficiency, invulnerability, not needing, not wanting anything or anybody. If this indeed is an attempted solution, then the implications for education may be considerable; after all, learning requires the acknowledgement of one's own vulnerability implicit in not knowing. One has to own up to not knowing before one can assimilate knowledge from another, with its implication of a lack in oneself. This may well reinforce any self-reproach associated with vulnerability or dependence, making it difficult to learn but also to communicate. Communication then happens indirectly, and in the adolescent's unease, or symptom, one has to excavate the psychological message:

> George, a strapping, if mute, 16 year old was brought to me by his concerned and exasperated father. He had been suspended from school after a number of violent and uncontrollable outbursts towards other pupils. He presented as sullen and resentful, whose main response to my questions and attempts to make contact was a curt 'Dunno', or, if I was lucky, as it implied some affective engagement, 'Boring'.
>
> The school was concerned that he showed no remorse about his actions, and he refused to talk to me or respond to questions about the events leading up to his suspension, or indeed to take up any prompting to talk about his feelings. These were all invitations to replicate his family and school situations, where he would be assiduously questioned either as a result of concern or coercion, merely putting George on the defensive, where his only recourse

was to withdraw into his shell of cultivated disinterest and indifference.

He continued to be brought by his father, and to be disaffectedly silent for some weeks before I commented, out of my own exasperation at our seemingly lifeless and void meetings, how odd it was that someone as old, physically mature and determined as himself should be brought to see me by his father, who happened to be small, frail and exceedingly voluble; the opposite of George, in other words. This elicited interest and it was not long before George was talking about how problematic it was having a father like that, but on the other hand his father had when younger introduced him to football. This was George's total preoccupation.

I now could not stop him talking about his favourite club, reciting their recent triumphs and how he himself was a player to be reckoned with; in this discourse I learnt, without either of us acknowledging that this was actually being said, that George hated losing. It was humiliating and involved a loss of face; it made him angry as it suggested some major deficit in himself. In actual fact he was tall, ungainly, and clumsy, which increased his desperation to be a winner. He had a sophisticated awareness of others who might be better than him, making him aware of his own limitations and leading him to ensure these players, and there were many, were ruthlessly tackled and prevented from shining. Essentially, despite his mature appearance, he was not sure whether he would ever be good enough himself; he needed to be better, tougher, and more belligerent to mask his insecurity and ensure that those perceived as better were 'ruthlessly' brought back to his level. If growing up means the tacit acknowledgment that others are different he was going to attempt to ensure that the debate occurred on his territory; out of a sense of inferiority *vis-à-vis* others he would ensure that they too would remain stuck, in this case at his level of footballing ability: a solution at once painful for his opponents as well as self-defeating for himself. Belligerence was an attempted denial of his perceived post-pubertal destiny, as well as an attempt to convince himself that he was as good, if not better, than the others, a debate which was in danger of being lost in George's internal world.

Communication, then, becomes an issue of recognizing metaphors; both parties know what is being said without its being talked about. Education, and an attitude towards learning, can be a metaphor in itself, where the latent context or purpose needs to be teased out from its manifest presentation.

Clearly, adolescence, like education, is not solely an intra-psychic or inter-personal event. In some ways quite the opposite: we cannot avoid puberty but we might be able to process adolescence in a less repressive fashion. If, as Bloss (1979) suggests, puberty '. . . is an act of nature, adolescence is an act of man', we need to wonder why contemporary Western man has contributed to making adolescence such a tempestuous voyage, rather than ensuring that the *Sturm und Drang* of puberty is made less stressful by societal structures. Conversely, one might conceive of having a different relationship to turbulence: if society viewed adolescent turbulence as a good thing – or looked upon it more benignly in the service of growing up – then we may become more concerned about conformity and compliance, which, not least in education, are seen as contemporary adolescent virtues.

During childhood our roles are ascribed to us by others, while at adolescence, as we attempt to free ourselves from ascription and develop an identity or role which feels comfortable for us, we are perhaps, perversely, most dependent on societal and cultural sign-posts to aid this voyage of self-and-other discovery. Our culture has defined adolescence as both lengthy and turbulent where rites of passage are difficult to discern. It is unclear how boys become men and girls women in Western societies other than by trial and error, while society itself appears confused as to what constitutes adulthood. If there is no such thing as society, how does one become a citizen? Almost imperceptibly, particularly in the secondary and higher field, education now acts as the primary rite of passage for young people, coinciding as it does with major psychological, physiological and cultural transitions. Perhaps because adolescence is such a confusing and problematic issue, challenging our spurious adult certainties, the management of adolescence has been delegated – at times it seems solely – to education.

As we shall see, at a time in a young person's life of overt and covert protest, education is in danger of demanding compliance and uniformity of thought, behaviour, and action. If, from what has been said, we see adolescence and young adulthood as periods where our developmental imperatives are to strive towards individuality yet sameness, necessitating behavioural and emotional experimentation, then it becomes apparent that these are qualities which are not easily accepted or understood in secondary and higher education. In a sense they are not syntonic with a contemporary form of learning which places a premium on regularity, conformity, and predictability. Education frequently demands more or less passive acceptance of both rules and ideas, which invite the possibility of a submissive compliance, which, as we shall see, carries with it the danger of leading to a form of pseudo-maturity, hollow in content; a psychological foreclosure. At a time when it might be more fruitful for us to rebel and test out the adult world, we may not be able to do this without seriously jeopardizing our educational careers.

Education can appear perplexed by adolescence, and helpless perplexity leads to a wish to manage or control it in some form of neatly observable fashion. In some measure education shares the psychological conundrum of adolescence: is adolescence by its very nature a 'problem' which needs to be 'cured' and tamed by education, or should education challenge the 'upholding of a steady equilibrium' (Freud, A., 1958) during adolescence since some form of confusion and turmoil appears a necessity for healthy development? The adolescent himself, requiring firmness and containment, while also room for manoeuvre and freedom to retain both distance and individuality, will share these doubts.

Psychoanalytic descriptions of adolescence, with their concentration on stages, transition, repetition, and separation, portray a process which, however turbulent, is frequently seen as manifestly static. The doldrums beckon, with their inevitable and interminable longeurs; we wait for something which is going to push us in some direction. However, there are no doldrums or contemporary moratoriums in our education system. Psychological concepts which base their descriptions of adolescence on the static nature of the period, may well not incorporate the fluidity or plasticity of the adolescent process nor take due account of the impact of external stresses on those years; education, for one, does not allow us to stand still.

Adolescent 'bumps'

There is a special rowing occasion in Oxford called Eights Week, more colloquially 'The Bumps'. This involves a large number of rowing boats, including rowers of all standards, starting a few boat lengths apart with the intention of bumping into the boat in front. This lasts over a period of a few days, and if you succeed in bumping the boat in front you take its place; if the boat behind you bumps into you, it takes your place. This strikes me as being a perfect metaphor for adolescence; you either get bumped into from behind (others push you forward or overtake you), or you bump into people ahead of you, whose place you then occupy at their expense. Nowhere is this process more evident than in education; you cannot stand still, or if you do you risk being bumped and overtaken. Adolescent students are continually exposed to the 'bumps'; they may wish to deny them, but they cannot ignore them. Frequently, being bumped will necessitate behaviours which at any other stage of life would appear strange and worrying.

Anna Freud pleas for a measure of adaptive 'abnormality' during adolescence, suggesting that the adolescent should risk behaving in an:

> . . . inconsistent and unpredictable manner, to fear his impulses and to accept them . . . to love his parents and to hate them . . . be deeply ashamed to acknowledge his mother before others, and unexpectedly, to desire heart to heart talks with her, to thrive on imitation and identification with others while searching increasingly for his own identity . . . Such fluctuations between such extreme positions would be deemed highly abnormal at any other time of life. At this time they may suggest no more than that an adult personality takes a long time to emerge. The adolescent must not cease to experiment and is in no way to close down on possibilities (Freud, A. 1958).

Experimentation often involves getting it wrong. Increasingly education is about getting things right. We are faced with this seemingly impossible contradiction; the developmental demands and preoccupations of late adolescence and early adulthood may well conflict with the demands education makes on us. What we may psychologically need to do in adolescence may well be at variance with what is expected of us in secondary, further, and higher education. The problem is that while we may be academically successful, we may fail in our personal and emotional development. The converse is also true of course; a preoccupation with our own unresolved psychological issues, without their being identified and addressed, may lead us to under-function if not opt, or drop, out.

In education we are faced with the need to allow adolescents enough scope to find themselves, while at the same time ensuring that that process is not self-destructive or a threat to others. We need time to allow our students to rebel or withdraw while at the same time standing firm, giving them something to rebel against or withdraw from. If we accept Winnicott's prescription for adolescence as essentially being about survival and containment, that is establishing a framework and environment that is safe enough for the adolescent to feel secure, the parent, and by implication the tutor or educational institution, needs to be able to take what is given without retaliating in kind or demanding a false and precocious compliance. Education is potentially well placed to respond, for this is what education at its best does; at a time of turbulence for the individual adolescent, and in an increasingly changing and complex world it optimally provides an island of continuity, predictability, and safety where academic and personal needs can be addressed and worked through.

For many adolescents educational institutions are now sanctuaries, the only safe place where these issues can be addressed. Adolescent creativity may well require the framework which only education can provide, a point movingly described by J.B. Pontalis (1993) when recalling his school days:

> It shouldn't be thought that I'm yielding here to some kind of nostalgia. There are whole pieces of childhood that arouse in me neither regret nor excitement. Or, if there is nostalgia, it's of a very particular nature: as far as the *lycée* is concerned, it is nostalgia for a world that was closed and minutely ordered but – within this enclosure, within this order, this regulated system – shot through with an extraordinarily open, fluid and varied life. Slogan for slogan, I would say: my *lycée* was Versailles.

We need education not merely to learn. If we can accept adolescence as a process, then the aim may be not merely to survive adolescence but to consolidate adolescence as a state of mind, as opposed to a stage, that one can have access to; it is less something one survives, or necessarily forgets, but something we continuously need to reflect and draw upon. Perhaps we need to find a verb for adolescence, say, 'adolescing', which does justice not only to the fluidity of our internal and external worlds during this period, but also describes a more general state of mind. Education, too, may need to be transposed into a verb; it is potentially less about needing knowledge for some functional end than a state of mind. The wish to be educated rather than the need for education is surely what creativity and learning are about. The demand to be educated at adolescence may well be society's attempt to cure and control the frightening post-pubertal eruption; in that it can only fail; where it may succeed is in respecting the adolescent process and speaking to its central anxieties.

In the following chapter we will look at how some of these issues are displaced onto and enacted in education and the process of learning when we decide to become students.

2
Transitions

I suppose it was the fear of drastically outdistancing my father that had caused me, in my first years at college, to feel as though I was something like his double or medium, emotionally to imagine that I was there at college on his behalf and that it wasn't just I who was being educated but him that I was delivering from ignorance as well. Just the opposite was happening of course. Every book I underlined and marginally notated, every course I took and paper I wrote was expanding the mental divide that had been growing wider and wider between us since I had prematurely entered high school at 12, just about the age that he had left school for good to help support his immigrant parents and all their children. Yet for many months there was nothing my reasonable self could do to stave off the sense of merging with him that overcame me in the library and in the classroom and at my . . . desk, the impassioned, if crazy, conviction that I was somehow inhabited by him and quickening his intellect right along with mine (Roth, 1991).

One of the central questions in education is: who are we studying for, and who are we attempting to educate? It is not always clear. By becoming educated are we enriching or depleting ourselves? Are we risking endangering our links with significant others, who have had an experience of the educational system and the process of learning before us?

The psychological project in education is always diverse and multifaceted, and coincides with a certain confusing ambiguity; is education something we want or need? There may be external pressures to be educated, but internal resistances: others may demand it of us but we may be reluctant to comply. While the explicit agenda is to learn, the student, of whatever age, will be seeking to address other, more personal and even secret scripts, which may well need to be acknowledged and dealt with before real learning can take place. If we view adolescence as a 'normative crisis' rather than a disease (Erikson, 1956), then the process of becoming and being a student is not a problem, requiring diagnosis and treatment, but a developmental obstacle which needs to be negotiated and surmounted.

The process of study allows development and education to coincide, and potentially to collide. For students, joining, performing and leaving mirrors not only issues in their own development, but also all of our life-cycles. As students study, it is not illogical to infer that it is in relation to the institution, their course and their teachers that these developmental preoccupations will be addressed.

A new framework

In Chapter 1 we looked at the developmental demands and preoccupations of late adolescence and early adulthood. These included the loss of home and childhood, physical maturational changes, gender identity, intimacy with peers, conflicts between dependence and autonomy, and the formation of an effective style of work and play. In education these will tend to be enacted within the academic task and more specifically in the process of learning. As a result of these transitions a young undergraduate will be faced with numerous challenges to their often fragile framework of home, school, and family. The loss of this external framework will inevitably place considerable pressure on the individual's internal coherence. These developmental imperatives are not only mirrored, but can be addressed through the metaphor of education. The interaction between the individual and the academic and social demands intrinsic to being a student ensures that these issues have to be faced. 'Getting through' an educational course becomes a metaphor for emotional and psychological development; the transition from childhood to adulthood. Joining a new, and frequently large and impersonal institution, engaging with and producing satisfactory work, reaching a balance between passive dependence and independent thought and mastery, sitting examinations and leaving, both demands of and propels the student into facing their own psychological development. How these obstacles are surmounted will in some way be dependent on how similar issues have been negotiated in the past. Beginnings may well bring with them a mixture of developmental hope, of moving on to something new and potentially exciting, while for some they may be infused with the fear of a repetition of an earlier failure. If previous beginnings have been frustrating, unsuccessful, or involved excessive amounts of loss, then the anxiety must be that the new setting will recapitulate the earlier experience. Just as we might be ambivalent about our own development, education is fused with similar hesitations and doubts; each step up the educational ladder brings with it new possibilities, not least independence and freedom, but also a lingering sense of what has been lost.

Some of the obstacles to learning in higher and further education are self-evident. Consequently, steps can be taken to counteract or at least to acknowledge them. Being able or successful in a school setting may not prepare you for being ordinary in a large university setting full of other able and successful students. Teaching methods and subjects are novel and potentially confusing. Idealization of the anticipated course and plan of study, coinciding as it does with the potential excitement of leaving home, may lead to disappointment and confusion with a potential search for scapegoats. Vulnerability may be dealt with by boisterous self-confidence or rebellion, while anxiety over social and academic competence may lead to withdrawal and depression. Some students may be reluctant to give up familiar and safe methods of studying or social relationships, with the consequent danger of denying that the new setting may call for different strategies:

James had diligently compartmentalized his life in the sixth form. Reading all the books on his book list for his holiday essays, eagerly anticipating prompt feedback from his teacher, while allowing himself one, parentally inspired, extra-curricular activity which gave some scope for interaction with other pupils. At university he was immediately confronted with three essays a week, book lists which were small novels in themselves, optional lectures and seminars, tutors who talked generally about his work without giving him a mark or indicating how he was doing, and the possibility of a social life which required some initiative and confidence on his part. He became over-anxious, confused, and bewildered in attempting to read everything on his book list, take copious notes in lectures (even attempting to tape record them when his writing could not keep up with the lecturer's pace), and unable to arrive at a considered judgement of how much time to allocate to work and how much to other activities, if only he could think of what they might be. Rather than seeing these issues as part of the transition process he was going through, he personalized them, became significantly depressed, and left his course.

Learning as a solution

Other obstacles are more diffuse. Is the decision to become a student a positive or negative one for that individual? Does university represent a compliance with another's need or wishes? Geographic separation from parents may provoke previously denied issues around emotional separations. Some students may find themselves quite advanced in their university careers before they question, possibly for the first time in their lives, why they are studying, and who the degree might be for. After all, 'getting to university' is a different project with a different set of demands than 'being at university'. For many students university has been their parentally or teacher-inspired goal. Studying then becomes a solution to someone else's demands; in a very real sense we are learning for another at some cost to the self. If university and 'being at' university is a perceived response to someone else's needs (or an imagined solution to a personal problem which 'getting to university' will cure), then it carries with it the danger of alienating the student from themselves and encouraging them to pursue a course not of their choosing. Are they at university for themselves, their parents, teachers, or for some family need? Or is it merely an acceptable excuse to leave home? The task for these students is to value what university can offer for themselves, rather than passively accept what others have told them of the value of a university education. Being unable to do this may lead some students to feel that not being able to adapt, fit in and perform reflects badly on them; it then becomes an alien demand which they cannot meet.

If obstacles '. . . [are] used to conceal unconscious desires . . . a way of not letting something else happen' (Phillips, 1993) then we cannot have obstacles without desire. If there are obstacles to study, then the associated if repudiated desire cannot be far away. In education obstacles are clues as to what we really want but feel we cannot or are not equipped to have. We may place them there as a way of thwarting others' impingements on ourselves, relentlessly cling to them as a means of communication, or we may ensure that the obstacle is a way of dealing with a desire that feels dangerously shocking:

> Madeline was an extremely able student coming to the end of her undergraduate career. She had worked hard and done well, but had become overwhelmed by anxiety lest her final examination mark failed to do justice to her hard work, and had become obsessed to the point of paralysis about obtaining a first-class degree. She was the eldest of four daughters and, as she had always been successful academically, had been viewed and called 'the brainbox' of the family. Madeline felt that her mother particularly had difficulty in viewing her in any other way, other than 'bright'. She was becoming concerned as to how she could continue to be the 'brain, for . . . I mean, of my mother . . . no . . . not of, I don't know what I mean' if she did not obtain a first-class degree.
>
> Her anxiety started when, as a result of continuous, migraine-like headaches, Madeline could not think. Not to be able to think carried with it the danger, albeit a seductively attractive one, of not existing for her mother. Her mother was perceived as being unable to view her in any other than a solely cerebral light, whereas there was really more to Madeline than that. What better obstacle, than to be truly mindless, existed for Madeline in her ambivalent attachment to her mother? If this was the only obstacle, then Madeline could have taken great neurotic pleasure in performing

less than perfectly in her final examinations. However, an additional complication was that Madeline was, despite being the eldest, still living at home, which enabled her to avoid the messy complications of the colleges' social life, and also to regulate her relationship with her boyfriend, who she saw at stipulated times during the week. Living at home meant there was no possibility of turning the relationship into a physical one. It eventually transpired that if she did not obtain a first, and thereby funding for a post-graduate course of study, Madeline would have to 'leave home, find a job, and possibly even get married'. Not getting a first was truly unthinkable. Beyond the obstacle of not being able to think, a serious handicap in (some) educational circles, lay the drive to escape from the mother/home, a desire fused with danger as Madeline found certain forms of gratification problematic.

We need to nurture our educational obstacles, as they communicate what cannot be said or only intermittently thought. If young adulthood is a period when we question previous generations' beliefs and values, then compliance, rebellion, or subversion become educational possibilities. For many, the only area, safe or otherwise, for subversion is the academic one. Academic failure in particular becomes a successful subversion – a necessary way of asserting autonomy, or a gesture of independence – and a displacement from other grievances. If getting a degree is a 'gift' or present for the parents or significant figures in the past, then should the student feel ambivalent towards these figures, or some element of developmentally appropriate reproach, the granting of the gift may be more complex; it may even at times be withheld. One could term this a developmental wish to fail.

For many students, being at university, but not being able to write essays or sit examinations, may be an unsatisfactory, if inevitable, compromise between compliance with a parental wish, albeit at the cost of some self-contempt, and subverting that wish as an expression of autonomy. Many may 'need' to be at university, but equally 'need' to withhold academic work. Freud said that the child's first successful lie to its parents was the first successful step to independence. At university, the lie, if only metaphorically, more often than not leads to either academic failure or its corollary, fear of success. Success can require one, as we have seen with Madeline, to leave home and enter the adult world.

Food for thought

The analogy between learning and food has been commented on at length (Salzberger-Wittenberg, 1983). The prototype for conflict-free digestion, whether in a mental or physical sphere, is the infant's relationship with its primary caretaker. This forms the basis of all later experiences of taking in, metabolizing, and giving back. To take in knowledge one has to have a certain enjoyment in being fed, not least a relationship of trust and curiosity towards knowledge or its physical manifestation: the teacher.

The balance between receptive dependence and active mastery, often in evidence in the working relationship between student and teacher, is rarely straightforward. The feelings of helplessness induced by not knowing may evoke the omnipotent belief that we know it all and do not need others. If our early experiences, perhaps with food, or its metaphoric equivalent, love, are fused with high levels of frustration and ambivalence, then the absence of a certain form of appetite for learning may be reflected in feelings of fear, distrust, or resentment. Learning may involve fantasies of inferiority and humiliation. We may wish to become mindless or empty when certain experiences become too painful to think about. Madeline's headaches would suggest that there are occasions when mental pain cannot be thought about, only experienced as a physical sensation or somatic event which may inhibit learning.

The role of depression

If higher education is a point of transition, then, as with all transitions, something can be both lost and gained. If learning involves a loss of innocence, then being at university may confront us with having to grieve our naive selves while at the same time being receptive to new experiences and knowledge which may be potentially overwhelming. Depression in students, as in adolescence, is not only ubiquitous, but also a potentially healthy adaptation to new psychic and environmental demands. Learning is closely associated with separation and loss. Knowing things may mean having to separate from those to whom we are still attached. Depressive under-functioning in a student may imply a successful submission or an attempt to protect us from the type of person that we fear, that is, wish, we might become, with its inevitable consequence of distancing ourselves from others to whom we have hitherto been close. Not knowing can be a way of avoiding separations. In this sense a depressive breakdown can be a breakthrough. Jeffrey is an example of this process of how separation, loss, and learning can become fused:

> Jeffrey, a 20-year-old second-year undergraduate physicist, was referred by his G.P., who described him as significantly depressed and becoming increasingly socially withdrawn – staying in his

room, not eating, and from time to time engaging in minor acts of self-harm (cutting his arm with a blunt knife). He was arousing a great deal of anxiety, with his G.P. wanting him to be seen by a counsellor as soon as possible, which contrasted with Jeffrey himself, who clearly did not want to be seen at all.

I was confronted by a pale, gaunt, ascetic young man, who clearly did not want to be either at university or in my consulting room. He was passive, morose, and significantly uncommunicative in the initial consultation. The story we laboriously pieced together ran as follows. As a result of his father's employment, the family moved frequently in his first few years before eventually settling in a small town in the north of England. He lived, seemingly uneventfully, with his parents and younger sister, until his father died suddenly when Jeffrey was 14. Jeffrey threw himself into his academic work, watched over by a mother who became increasingly 'pushy'. He did not want to be at university, and suspected nefarious forces were conspiring to push him here: he thought his mother had an informal link with his college. While academically successful in his first year, he consciously avoided making new friendships or taking part in the many activities which university had to offer. Interestingly, what was very striking in his description of his current life was that he would have nothing to do with anything associated with the university, but would occasionally attend social events in the town which appeared to give him the comfortable yet not wholly pleasant experience of maintaining an identification with home.

He was angry and dismissive of the 'ritual pomp/stuffiness' of university life, and wanted nothing to do with it. He continued with a desultory relationship with a girlfriend at home, who only appeared to provide comfort and relief from his sufferings at university rather than any substantial pleasure; it also, of course, gave him reason not to engage in any social activities in college. He was becoming disinterested in work, but felt trapped. He was almost compelled to 'be here' but did not want to be – it was interesting at this point that I was unclear whether he was referring to university or the consulting room. It will come as no surprise to learn that he was also passive and reluctant to engage in the process of therapy, other than to be in the consulting room. When I commented on this, he mentioned being temperamentally shy and self-effacing, 'a bit like my father'.

His father had attended a provincial university and hated it. Eventually, Jeffrey thought his father had worked himself to death doing something he did not enjoy. It was as though Jeffrey was at university for his father, not only because he was doing something without enjoyment, but also because while it was his mother who was experienced as being the 'pushy', university-oriented parent, he believed his father would have been quietly proud of him. But in order to maintain an identification with him, Jeffrey took great pains to both dislike the place, and avoid engaging in anything associated with it, which might be fatal; for by engaging with it he ran the risk of betraying his father's memory. His impotent anger and resentment, turned primarily against the self, was something he could not let go of; it was a perverse way of keeping his father alive in a moribund state. His dead father accompanied him everywhere. He knew his father did not like physics either, and would, had he been alive, known exactly what Jeffrey felt. Nostalgia for the 'uneventful' childhood days before his father's death was palpable.

Jeffrey could not let go of his resentment because it combined an attack on himself via his detachment (an unconscious equation of working hard and being in the world = killing people); resentment of others (who had live fathers, or mothers who had been unable to keep fathers alive); as well as maintaining an identification with a father in fantasy who hated university, would have been proud of him, but was dead. Living and learning would mean psychologically burying his father and coming to terms with the loss.

Envy

Further obstacles to study may include unease in the area of rivalry, competition, and envy. As learning requires some degree of active mastery, students' relationship to their own assertiveness, competition, and sense of active potency will affect the degree to which academic demands are met. Alleged laziness may reflect key discomfort with one's own aggression, which can be perceived as potentially too destructive. Conversely, since most learning occurs in groups, one's peers are inevitably one's rivals. We cannot be the same as everyone else, even though we might attempt to be so; we are always, subjectively at least, better or worse. Inhibitions, or lack of them, in these areas will inevitably have some academic consequences.

Because we are always potentially made vulnerable by others who know or have more, envy, as distinct from the wish to emulate, is a constant factor in education. This can take the form of envy in relation to another – an example would be the student's envy of the teacher's superior knowledge and status, which carries with it the danger of academic paralysis or an attack on the other. Alternatively, envy can become a subjectively perceived obstacle to our own success:

Susan, a bright and attractive final-year student at a prestigious university consulted me six months before the completion of her four-year course, wanting to leave, feeling desperately miserable, and unable to enjoy either studying or her hitherto active social life. She was a gregarious and attractive young woman, who was able for long periods of her studies to 'forget' about her family back home. Mother and father, neither of whom had been to university, lived with Susan's two younger sisters, who clearly were not as able or presentable as she. She had begun to feel miserable and 'blocked' when writing an essay in her literature course on women's aspirations, which she had failed to complete. She complained of a pervasive feeling of inadequacy and fraudulence, which had the unintended consequence of leading her to 'think more about her family', which, strangely for her, was experienced as comforting. It transpired that she feared her own imminent success would outstrip that of her family, particularly her parents, hence the need to forget, which produced an overwhelming feeling of guilt. Despite her parents' objective pleasure at her success, Susan experienced a vague feeling of unease, almost a fear of retaliation; she frequently felt persecuted by thoughts of her own imminent downfall, and how well deserved that may be. How better, then, not to graduate, rejoin the ranks of her family, and, as a punishment for her own hubris, allow her younger and possibly envious sisters to take centre stage in the quest for success.

Success may court an envious attack, particularly if you have been or felt to be the most enviable child. An envious attack need not originate from outside the self. Successful students are often the most enviable of children, and since envy has a persecutory flavour to it, both envier and envied come to fear it. The envier attempts to negate and destroy the envied, while the envied is always in danger of subverting the self in an attempt to ward off or deal with the envious attack. As envy is intrinsically opposed to creativity, it is inevitable that it is never far from the surface in our attitudes to learning. Teaching relationships are not immune from envy in offering a choice between insulating ourselves from the other or attempting to negate, mock, or destroy the source of the envious discomfort. If our envy is too pervasive, we may not be able to contemplate taking things in from the outside out of a fear that they are dangerous and may harm us. The attempt to turn knowledge into 'rubbish' is an example of this, and ensures that we avoid incorporating into ourselves something so pernicious; better to be empty than full of malignant nonsense.

If receiving a university education is the preserve of the few, then envy is in danger of being sanctioned and reinforced. Can the small, ostensibly privileged minority allow themselves to succeed, and if so, who, if anyone, is being betrayed? We may well have complex feelings about those who have not succeeded and who we have left behind. The university student may have to come to terms with the guilt consequent upon the triumphant excitement on obtaining a place in higher education, particularly if places are perceived as exclusive. How do we make sense of ourselves in relation to those who we have left behind?

Linda, a student at the end of her first year, consulted me after a series of panic attacks when she would find herself hyperventilating, feeling nauseous, shaking, and tearful. These occurred in public places in the college, and would necessitate Linda retreating to her room for days on end, fearing a repetition of the attacks if she ventured out.

During my initial meetings with her a frequent theme in her discourse was betrayal: by a boyfriend for summarily leaving her, by her tutor for seemingly becoming increasingly disinterested in her academic progress, and by her few friends, who she accused of disloyalty. She was, even at this early stage in her studies, anxious about leaving, and dealt with this by a certain determination not to make any 'lasting' friendships as these would inevitably lead to disappointment. She worked hard, plagued by an internal mother who would 'accuse' her of enjoying herself on the few occasions she took part in other activities.

Linda was preoccupied by needing to 'repay' all those who had supported her in getting to university; her parents and her extended family. She came from a small, closely knit mining community many miles from the university, and was the first of her family to go to university, the only one of her classmates to achieve that distinction. It gradually became apparent that the betrayal lay not in others but in herself. Linda felt ill at ease, panicky even, at university as its values, ethos and culture were so different from home, and was plagued by the need to work – after all, it was the only reason she, and her internalized parents, believed she was at college. And yet the more work she did, the more alienated she felt from all that home represented; she was betraying her past and was feeling progressively alienated both from the world of her family and her new college world, which felt insubstantial, yet held out the promise of a potentially interesting other life. Linda was trapped between the world of her past, familiar and yet increasingly distant, and her present life to which she had to maintain an air of distrust lest her 'parents suspect' she may be enjoying it. For Linda, enjoyment implied that she was jettisoning all that they represented.

Where higher education is not synonymous with our pasts, we may panic in attempting to bridge the ever-increasing chasm which education may represent. Learning may damage the health of others and lead to students having to deal with a sense of hubris, contempt, and disloyalty towards their parents, or their backgrounds.

Leaving home

Just as in adolescence, where the young person and their family need to mourn the passing of a developmental stage, the same is true for parents when a student leaves home for college. How a student manages this transition is in part a consequence of how facilitating the family have been, which in turn depends on how the family are able to incorporate change during this period. If families are uneasy about the departure of the young person they may consciously or unconsciously resist separation, making the consequent mourning, and the resolution of that process, impossible. This in turn will affect how the young person settles into a college environment. They may feel they do not have permission to either succeed or to become more successful than their parents. Attachment to their new environments may become fraught with ambivalence. An all-too-easy compromise to this dilemma is to proceed with a parentally approved course and then fail. University may be seen as a possible solution to this dilemma, only in the event to disappoint. The student may worry what is going on at home in their absence. Are their parents managing without them? Will they be missed? Will a sibling take their place? What is happening to their room? The first vacation is often the time when the realization is made that despite the familiarity of their surroundings, nothing will ever be the same again.

Parents may be resistant on various levels to the separation, not least if the potential student had been used to conceal marital tensions. There then may be covert attempts to prevent separations. The student may show signs of unease, necessitating the parents to become involved again. Conversely, the student may be required to become reinvolved with the parents again if their marriage begins to falter (a not unusual occurrence at a time when the young person leaves for university), or become pulled back into the family nexus by a parent who becomes ill on the young person's departure. The student may feel either prematurely deserted by the parents or surreptitiously held on to; both can lead to resentment which may be displaced on to the academic arena.

A common occurrence is where parents attempt to resolve their own unfulfilled ambitions by exerting vicarious pressure on their offspring. Students may be encouraged to become extensions of their successful parents and propelled to emulate, often in the same field, at the same educational institution, the parents' success. Students are in danger of joylessly failing in this attempt to become like someone else, or giving up altogether. Dogged commitment to a field or place of study solely to fulfil a parental wish becomes a demand which the student meets with either resentful compliance or less resentful subversion. Conversely, parental envy at the student's success can have an equally unfortunate outcome. On these occasions it is unclear whose need to be educated is being met. Academic achievement or lack of it becomes the arena where unresolved conflicts with parents are played out.

A special re-enactment

For students who are negotiating these obstacles it becomes self-evident that 'the tutor' will at times come to symbolically represent and be used as something other than merely the teacher. Since tutors, whether they encourage this or not, will inevitably have ascribed to them the position of representing the individual to the institution and the institution to the individual student, they will court a certain form of attachment. The tutor will be walking a tightrope, invited to identify with either the individual or the institution – another example of the ubiquitous if fallacious demand in education to choose between two opposites, when the need may be to choose neither, but to act as a 'transitional space' in facilitating student and institution communicating and listening to each other.

Inevitably, developmental issues such as autonomy or dependence become apparent in the tutorial relationship. How comfortable does the student feel being taught, with its invitation to take up a dependent position, while the psychological imperative, as we have seen, may be to become independent? Being independent may well conflict with allowing oneself to be taught by others who know more. Pernicious envy can lead people to sabotage or spoil what might otherwise be a good learning experience. Conversely, if developmental anxiety leads us to remain dependent and avoid adult responsibility, learning is in danger of being defined as passively accepting knowledge from the tutor.

With remarkable prescience, Freud (1914) commented on the inevitability of turning our teachers into our own subjective creations, irrespective of their intrinsic qualities or who they are. What they evoke in us and what we see in them, becomes instrumental in how we seek to use them:

> . . . the individual's emotional attitudes to other people, which are

of such extreme importance to his later behaviour, are already established at such an early age. The nature and quality of the human child's relation to people of his own and his opposite sex have already been laid down in the first six years of his life. He may afterwards develop and *transform* [my italics] them in certain directions but can no longer get rid of them. The people to whom he is in this way fixed are his parents and his brothers and sisters. All those whom he gets to know later, become *substitute* [my italics] figures for these first objects of his feelings ... His later acquaintances are thus obliged to take over a kind of emotional heritage; they encounter sympathies and antipathies to the production of which they themselves have contributed little.

In the same paper, Freud's preoccupation with fathers led him to see them as the mutative objects for substitution and transformation:

In the second half of his childhood, a change sets in in the boy's relation to his father ... From his nursery the boy begins to cast his eyes upon the world outside. And he cannot fail to make discoveries which undermine his original high opinion of his father and which expedite his detachment from his first ideal ... he finds that his father is no longer the mightiest, wisest and richest of beings; he grows dissatisfied with him; he learns to criticize him ... and then ... makes him pay heavily for the disappointment that has been caused by him ... It is in this phase of the youth's development that he comes into contact with his teachers. So that we can now understand our relation to our schoolmasters. These now ... become our substitute fathers ... we *transferred* on to them the respect and expectations attaching to the omniscient father of our childhood, and we then began to treat them as we treated our fathers at home. We confronted them with the ambivalence that we had acquired in our own families, and ... we struggled with them as we had been in the habit of struggling with our fathers. Unless we take into account our nurseries and our family homes our behaviour to our schoolmasters would not only be incomprehensible but inexcusable.

Even allowing for elements of paternal determinism in the early Freud, this is remarkable for a number of reasons. We are immediately made aware of the possibility that just as we think we are leaving our family and its familiar dynamics behind, we are unconsciously or occasionally consciously recreating it in any putative learning setting. We thought we had escaped something only to be instrumental in re-enacting it in our studies, and in our relationship to our tutors and fellow students, who may come to represent our estranged siblings. Equally, Freud alerts us to the fact that we may use our tutors ruthlessly in pursuit of our own developmental imperatives. Tutors can become (un)willing participants in the ensuing dance. The legacies of family life are enacted with unsuspecting tutors, who are made into something they are not: potential objects of love, idealization, denigration, fear, hatred, ridicule, and envy. The implication is that the student will leave the family home and approach the unfamiliar world, including people and situations, on the basis of expectations and fantasies derived from home (Freud, A., 1955).

Transference

Freud also alerts us to the impending discovery of the mechanics of this *transfer* and *substitution*; transference and its vicissitudes. Transference encompasses both the belief and the process that feelings and attitudes connected with the past are experienced and re-enacted in current relationships. If indeed our childhood experiences were of harsh, critical parenting we may anticipate this form of relating from our tutors. If parenting was experienced as lax and indulgent we may again be expecting to set up a familiar dynamic with our tutors and become uneasy and bewildered if this is not possible.

In the history of psychoanalysis, transference was initially seen as an obstacle which would impede the therapeutic task (or, one might imply, teaching) before being viewed more positively as a major therapeutic agent. The psychoanalytic patient would repeat in relation to the analyst as a contemporary experience something which otherwise would be forgotten or only dimly remembered as belonging to the past; the therapeutic task then became converting the repetition into something that can be reflected on and thought about, rather than enacted.

Transference shifted from being an obstacle to being a therapeutic tool in the consulting room at the same time as psychoanalytic theory was moving from being quasi-biological, occupied with 'instincts and drives', to being much more concerned with our capacity to form relationships with others. It may well be that in tutorial relationships the same shift is evident. If learning and teaching are less about an individual's cognitive capacities, and more about how we allow ourselves to use certain forms of relationships, then the transference to tutors becomes an important factor which need not impede the academic task. Its appearance, however, may well make that task more problematic, and if not acknowledged lead to a very different script being enacted. Its acknowledgement may facilitate a form of learning which has the potential for incorporating both academic and psychological development. By being able to recognize and not become overly collusive – that is, not fitting in with unrealistic or exaggerated expectations the student may have of them – or anxious – by either taking fright or negating the manifestations of a particular form of transfer – the tutor may well be able to expedite learning rather than reinforce what might initially be seen as an obstacle.

Examples of the transference process in education are widespread. Transference can affect:

> . . . (a) the way we perceive, (b) the way we interpret, (c) the way we behave. An example of (a) is of a boy who adores his mother and has been the apple of her eye. He may expect to seduce his teacher (as he did his mother) by his charm rather than feel a need to earn praise by hard work and achievement. An example of (b) is of a girl who has an ailing father and who interprets her teacher's absence invariably as a sign that she has been too much of a burden on him. An example of (c) is a young man who, expecting punishment, behaves so outrageously that he eventually drives his teacher to act in a punitive manner (Salzberger-Wittenberg et al., 1983).

The reality of the tutor is not an insuperable obstacle to the creation of this form of transfer. However, a consequence of the temptation offered by the transference is for the tutor to collude with a certain way of responding to the student, particularly if this involves idealization or various forms of seduction. A danger exists that a genuine bewilderment on behalf of the tutor can promptly turn into unease, anxiety, and annoyance when they are made into something they are not. Being turned into an ogre, the tutor may become one. For example, the student who persistently withholds a piece of work is encouraging the tutor to become intrusively demanding. Conversely, out of a wish to deny ogre-like qualities, tutors might find themselves becoming indulgent or seductive – the tutor who chooses to ignore the non-appearance of work or attempts to create a tutorial relationship with the student based upon a spurious and self-evidently lacking bonhomie. In education an attempt to turn the tutorial relationship into something totally other is an occupational hazard. There are as many scripts available for the tutorial relationship as there are students and tutors able to willingly or not enact them. This cannot be avoided, as tutors in their capacities to both nurture and judge students will inevitably evoke memories of objects in the student's past who fulfilled both those roles.

In order to create these transfer relationships we need to profoundly misunderstand or deny the real or actual situation. Just as the neurotic transference of the consulting room is a specific form of illusion – we can repeat without remembering – the transfer invited by the tutorial relationship offers the student the opportunity to repeat a certain form of relating in a context where that may be both inappropriate and impede learning. An educational setting which takes this into account can potentially establish a more creative and developmentally appropriate way of both relating and learning.

> The student who consulted me as a result of her concern that her tutor was intrusive, demanding, over-critical, preoccupied, and, she suggested, disliked her, and who replied, some time later, to my invitation to tell me a little about her family, that her father was intrusive, demanding, over-critical, preoccupied and disliked her, was able to obtain considerable relief from the recognition that she had constructed similarities, on the basis of little evidence, in a situation which was objectively, replete with difference.

The academic agenda can be subverted by a fantasy based on a subjective agenda, in which attitudes to authority, intimacy, cooperation or rivalry may not be shared in the tutorial dyad. The relationship then assumes a somewhat unreal and magical quality. Just as in Freud's case history of the Wolf Man, where his patient's inhibition to learning, ostensibly as a result of his teacher's negative attention, revived persecutory and destructive fears from early childhood, this illusory transfer relationship cannot be successfully enacted without the willing or unknowing participation of another. The student will seek out a suitable object with whom to enact these often unconscious and unresolved difficulties. To be able to do so clearly requires some indication that the object will, if not readily, comply (although sometimes the compliance meets a psychological need in the other), and at least unconsciously collude and accept if not encourage the subjective script.

Tutors too can transfer emotional baggage on to the students, and can, since rivalry, competition, identification, loving and hating are not prerogatives of the student role, become active participants in establishing and maintaining this illusory relationship. For example, tutors need to ensure that envy does not become an obstacle; they need to feel comfortable sharing the knowledge that they have with their students, without a grudging resentment that their knowledge is being stolen from them. Equally, since tutors have parents, they may find aspects of being *in loco parentis* a potentially uncomfortable and conflicted experience. Tutors who harbour unconscious, childlike hostility towards their parents are likely to identify with potentially childish desires in their students.

Counter transference

Just as the issue of transference has developed in psychoanalytic theory from being an obstacle to being something which is potentially facilitative, so too with its obverse: counter-transference. Whereas transference tends to emphasize a process occurring in the patient, counter-transference pays more attention to the relationship which exists between patient and therapist – for our purposes the student and tutor. In a generic sense counter-transference can be loosely used to describe the totality of the tutor's feelings towards the student. In this context, just as students do not arrive *tabula rasa* to their tutors, so too tutors harbour hopes, fears, and expectations in their tutorial encounters.

After initially being seen as a hindrance (the therapist's feelings get in the way with the task), aspects of the counter-transference are now increasingly viewed as a major therapeutic tool. Initially viewed as the opposite of the patient's transference, and therefore a potential blind spot (in education an example would be tutors who are uneasy about and have not resolved difficulties in relation to, say, aggression, may find themselves placating their students or retaliating in kind when they perceive them as hostile) counter-transference is now viewed as a method of communication.

The therapist or tutor may be the object of an affective state which has been placed in them by the patient/student. In this sense counter transference includes the possibility of an emotional communication. The need is then for therapist/tutor to tease out whether the discomfort is located in themselves (i e something in the discourse which makes them uncomfortable), or whether it is telling them something about that particular patient/student, and may be a means of gaining some insight into the other's communication or behaviour. If we accept that communication may not merely involve words, when tutors get, say, irritated by a particular student at a particular time, the need is to discover whether that tells them something about themselves, or whether it is a way in which the student is making themselves known.

Projection and projective identification

Emotions do not need words to be communicated; they too can be transferred. The mechanisms most commonly used for the transfer are projection and projective identification. An example of the former would be the student who for whatever personal reason transfers both the wish to learn and inquiring curiosity on to the unsuspecting tutor, who then is left to carry sole responsibility for the learning process. In this instance what has been projected, which can be an unacceptable wish, emotion or quality, is something unacceptable to the subject and consequently safely placed in the object who is then unconsciously invited to act out the projection.

Projective identification is a similar process with the addition that what is projected into the object is unconsciously intended to harm, possess, control, or communicate with the other. It can be a particularly malign form of identification, which impedes learning. What has been projected in this instance is part of the subject's self (aggression or depression, say) which the object then is left to experience. In the example quoted above the tutor would be left with disquieting, and possible hostile or depressive, feelings associated with the process. In attempting to evacuate something intolerable an attempt is made to control it in the other person. The student who places omniscient knowledge into the tutor so that the tutor knows everything may not merely be diminishing themselves, or their capacity to be knowledgeable, but also attempting to control omniscient knowledge and what it symbolically represents by placing it in the other person. In this example the tutor is in danger of feeling extremely uncomfortable. What is evacuated need not be all bad; we can also expel good things. An example would be our capacity for altruism when the tutor is experienced as too benign, leaving us feeling unworthy of such attention. These mechanisms are not mutually exclusive, or solely the prerogative of the tutorial relationship:

> Liz consulted me after a period where her academic work had been progressing poorly. Her tutor had appeared indifferent, and she subsequently arranged to have two tutors – one male, one female – to supervise different aspects of her studies, which provided some relief for her. However, the tutors had considerable difficulty negotiating between themselves regarding Liz's workload and academic commitments, which enabled Liz to both stand apart from their arguments (if not subtly encourage each to misunderstand the other) and receive considerable comfort from the ensuing confusion and squabbling over her academic welfare. At least neither tutor could be accused of indifference.
>
> It was only considerably later that I learnt that her parents had separated during Liz's early teens after many years of hostile disharmony, which took the form of neither talking to the other, with Liz being used as a neutral intermediary. The recreation of an acrimonious dyad enabled Liz to turn it into the form of triangular relationship, which, although manifestly disharmonious, was familiar. It enabled her to feel that she was being attended to as

indifference was her major anxiety: she had clearly picked up that her parents' use of her as an intermediary during her post-pubertal years was in a profound way a reflection of their indifference to her. To have her tutors passionately differ on her behalf recreated the familiar trauma, but fulfilled some reparative function, as she and her studies became central to her tutors' disagreements. Furthermore, Liz had a boyfriend who, with Liz's seemingly unconscious encouragement, entered into an ostensibly illicit, casual, sexual relationship with her best friend who subsequently accused him of assault. Liz's reaction was to split her loyalties: while encouraging her best friend to bring charges of assault against her boyfriend, with him she was solicitous and understanding, even to the extent of accompanying him to the police station and standing his bail. Her loyalties and identification were split. While ostensibly wanting to be reunited with her boyfriend, she was encouraging steps to be taken which would ensure the inevitable breakdown of the relationship. In being the active instigator of these various scripts, she was encouraging others to be the unwitting participants, and re-enacting an earlier trauma in a manner which was more controllable.

Transference and similar mechanisms imply the existence of a relationship between self and other. In the next chapter we will look at whether we need others to think, learn, and remain curious, and, if so, how this can be applied to the field of education. But first we need to think about thinking.

3
Thinking and development

It is hard to decide whether what affects us more and was of greater importance to us was our concern with the sciences that we were taught or with the personalities of our teachers . . . it is true . . . that this second concern was a perpetual undercurrent in all of us, and that in many of us the path to the sciences led only through our teachers (Sigmund Freud, 1914).

Transference to our teachers may facilitate learning, but do we need others to sustain our curiosity? Our identity, or sense of self, cannot exist in a vacuum, so our enjoyment of knowledge may depend on the nature and quality of the relationships which we allow ourselves, or are allowed, to establish. Can we educate ourselves without recourse to others? What are the factors which facilitate or hinder our capacity to remain curious and receptive to learning?

In the previous chapters we have concentrated on the factors which may interfere with learning. In this section we shall examine some of the factors which encourage learning, and ask whether the capacity to be receptive to new ideas is in itself a developmental achievement of some significance. Students study – but what does this mean? Is learning solely a cerebral activity? Thinking, as opposed to thoughts, may not come naturally.

In order to approach these questions we need to look at developmental theory and what it tells us about how we learn and perceive the world. Are problems of development, and by definition learning, relational or intrinsic to the self? That is, are relations between people of more importance in fostering thinking and learning than what happens inside them? If, as we shall see, infants are increasingly seen as active in relating to their environment, then developmental theories which rely on the premise of the passivity of the baby, and that development consists of filling up an empty shell from the outside, will have little to offer theories of education or how we learn.

The Freudian infant

Psychoanalytic investigations into development began – as a consequence of their need to present themselves as quasi-biological theories – with a baby who was full of drives and instincts which needed discharge. Thus the Freudian baby seeks out others for instinctual discharge and satisfaction as a way of mastering a potentially frustrating environment. Consequently, what we see is a baby searching for possible gratifications confronted with an environment seeking to guide the infant's attempts to use it in the pursuit of its own pleasure. By implication education would then involve attempts to coerce or channel the child into accepting the inevitability of its more impressive frustrations. In an essentially one-person psychology, the parent or teacher would stand apart from the process, merely influencing it as and when required. Inevitably, within this framework the infant is viewed either as a *tabula rasa* to be filled from the outside by whatever the environment chooses, or a cluster of instincts and desires which need to be tamed and socialized. Baby and environment are seen as two separate entities, interacting as and when necessary, but rarely if ever part of a relationship where one might influence the other.

The social infant

As psychoanalysis moved away from its biological origins towards a more explicitly psychological framework involving two- and three-person relationships, the concept of the social infant who has a relationship with itself and others from birth, and for whom issues of attachment were central, became the paradigm of developmental theory.

These ideas have become fundamental in current thinking about what fosters or hinders learning. The concept of mutually reciprocal influence is one that is now widely accepted: one party acts on and influences the other, but is also acted on and influenced by the other. 'At this very early state, it is not logical to think of an individual . . . If you set out to describe a baby, you will find that you are describing a "baby" and someone. A baby cannot exist alone but is essentially part of a relationship' (Winnicott, 1964). The Freudian baby is no longer shaped merely by physiological needs, which seek gratification, but is an active participant in creating and influencing its world; mother and child can reciprocally influence each other over and above the satisfaction of basic physiological needs.

Thus, relationships which involve the infant actively contributing to its environment become mutually sustaining and potentially gratifying. The implication therefore is that we are innately curious about others, rather than turning to others either for instinctual relief or grudgingly out of a despairing recognition that we cannot meet all our needs ourselves. Our concern with and for others is then a primary preoccupation rather than a consequence of our awareness of any possible benefits they may hold for us. Learning can then be mutually gratifying, rather than something that will make up for a narcissistic deficit or lack in ourselves.

The active infant

Recent research (Stern, 1985) has shown that newborns are interested in and respond to their environments from birth. Rather than being passive receptacles, infants are active participants in shaping their environments. As a consequence, the debate has shifted from an enquiry as to how we can best 'fill up' the *tabula rasa* of the unsuspecting infant, to a consideration of the obstacles preventing the infant from continuing to actively explore its environment. It is suggested that the infant will have picked up at the intra-uterine stage a particular aesthetic of its environment and the potential relationships on offer from maternal behaviour and preoccupations. These will form a template, or pre-transference, towards the idea of a social relatedness from birth. Prior to its birth, the unborn baby may have ascribed to it individual characteristics – even a personality – as a result of the interaction between parental expectation and the baby's active impact through movement, arousal, or mobility on its parents and surroundings.

This early relationship may be based on 'mutual delusions' (Brazelton and Cramer, 1991), but no less real for that; the infant and its immediate environment are introduced into the world of 'intersubjectivity' where through the interaction of the two a space is created for being in the world. Arguably no baby arrives without a pre-existing relationship in fantasy to both the world and its mother, which, while possibly magical in form and full of projective expectations, may pre-date its birth. The infant then becomes – and more importantly has the capacity to view itself as – an active participant in any exchange. The baby can experience itself as its own subject capable of influencing and being influenced by the object. Learning then becomes an interactional process where one participant can influence the other, and vice versa.

As a consequence of being an active participant, the infant has the capacity for a mode of learning that is not merely based on imitation, emulation, or thoughtless incorporation. The advantages of, for example, reading or writing for a child stem from a recognition that interaction – and having something to say – is of value as a result of its experience of being an active participant, i.e. and having a say in these forms of communication from an early age. Reading and writing, seen in this light, may be a way we separate and hold on to our parents. Because the baby cannot speak it does not follow that it has nothing to say or cannot communicate.

Separate and different

If from the beginning there are always two subjects, then learning is placed on the continuum of similarity and difference. Are we the same or different from the other? The successful parent – and the infant who is able to use an idiom of parenting successfully – depends on finding both similarities (a healthy use of projective identification as a mode of benign empathy) and noticing differences (an objective ability to stand outside and apart from the baby or parent) in the emerging relationship. The problem is not one of developing separateness, which is there from the beginning, but of acknowledging similarities in a relationship composed of individuals who are fundamentally different. Learning and teaching may need to be seen in the same paradigm.

One of the problems with earlier psychoanalytic theories of development is that development has predominantly been seen as progressing from oneness to separateness. Stern questions Mahler's (1975) – and by definition much psychoanalytic developmental theory – attachment to phases of development devoted to specific tasks, believing if there is an emergent self from birth then there cannot be any age-specific sensitive phases of development – particularly in relation to issues of trust, separation, autonomy and differentiation – merely issues for 'the life-span' which are continually accessible to be reworked at any age. The implication of this is a welcome liberation from psychoanalytic developmental determinism. It may be that reciprocity is more fundamental than either instinctual gratification or the gradual development of separateness. If there is no longer an autistic stage of development, and we are separate from the beginning, development hinges on how we negotiate our separateness from others while still remaining related and interdependent with them. Brazelton and Cramer (1991) contend that the concept of 'fusion', much in evidence in psychoanalytic theory, can no longer be viewed as a physiological reality, but more a psychological state which is problematic to relinquish. Physiologically we have always been separate, but need to go to great lengths to deny that to ourselves. This stands analytic theory on its head: the implication is that there is no primary state of autism or narcissism – we are always (and have always been) in relation to someone or something – but create fusion – or merging experiences – as a defence against the recognition of a primary separateness. Symbiosis may be a state of mind created to prevent us thinking about being different.

Development which proceeds linearly from oneness to separateness denies the possibility that it is only via the interrelation between the two that growth and learning occurs. In that sense we grow within relationships rather than out of them. If it is true that the infant is never undifferentiated, but from the beginning in a relationship with and curious in the outside world, the issue is not how we become independent of another, but how we negotiate our relationships. This may be a welcome development for psychoanalytic theory and practice, and also has implications for education. While maternal care and separation were seen as the fulcrum of a linear and progressive development, our lives were placed firmly in the field of nurture rather than desire. If we have received enough of the former, we will not be troubled by the latter. Consequently our need to separate from our mothers will always lead us to be ambivalent about nurture. Desire undergoes no similar transformation, making it more often than not a secret source of gratification.

Mother/child, teacher/student

The tutorial relationship, increasingly described as a form of mothering, i.e. nurture, has courted the same ambivalence between pleasurable protection and impingement in its students, leading the process of studying to being something we need rather than want. The possibility of seeing the tutorial relationship as one in which both student and teacher can be subject as well as object, each influencing the other, may serve to liberate the teaching relationship from some of its more problematic oppressive overtones. Teacher and tutee, like mother and baby, need each other in order to function: you cannot have one without the other. The question is no longer how you can deliver education to a passive child or student but how to harness the child's – or student's – innate curiosity and spontaneity in a joint project of learning. The student – like the newborn baby – may merely be searching for its capability and assertion to be recognized. This relational, as opposed to instinctual, model of development also implies that differing modes and levels of learning (emotional, social, cognitive) occur simultaneously. Splitting of function (intellect/emotion, teacher/taught) is avoided, and the person's need for the nourishment of getting to know someone is as important as their getting to know something.

If mutual influence and the capacity for recognition exist from the beginning, then clearly we can be over- or under-whelmed by the other. Too much or too little leads to a need for the interaction to be regulated in order that both parties can experience the other in manageable doses. Learning and teaching, like parenting and being parented, will involve oscillations between satisfaction and frustration, spontaneous enthusiasm and persistent effort.

The art of thinking

A similar process can be involved in thinking, or the capacity to have thoughts. We all have thoughts – they come naturally – but whether they lead to a process called thinking may be determined by our interaction with another. Thoughts are solipsistic, but it takes two to think. Thoughts come before thinking. Thoughts require the provision of an apparatus for them to be converted into a process called thinking. Thinking, as Wilfred Bion (1990) has said, 'has to be called into existence to cope with thoughts'. The implication is that at least initially thinking is not something we can do for ourselves. For Bion, 'thought has to emerge and cannot be forced into consciousness through artificial induction.' To be able to think, as opposed to having thoughts, may be a developmental achievement of the highest order requiring the assistance of another. If thinking is an accomplishment, then one can infer that there may be times when we would prefer not to think for ourselves, and to have our thinking done for us. People, says Bion, may be reluctant to think, or as he puts it, 'learn from experience', and prefer, like in a supermarket, to 'pick up a ready-made item (or thought) from the shelf.' Thinking may for whatever reason be painful, and as real learning requires thought, we might need to go to great lengths to resist it.

Magical thinking

How then are thoughts generated? If the origin of thought lies in infancy, then the capacity for creative thinking may be associated with early experiences of recognition, nurture, and taking things in from the outside – that is, feeding. In Freud's 1912 paper 'Formulations on the Two Principles of Mental Functioning' the infant, faced with unrequited hunger, becomes frustrated and responds to this by developing a form of 'hallucinatory wish-fulfilment' – a form of magical denial that it is either not hungry or that it can feed itself – which Freud believed was a primitive form of almost sensory thought. This provides some relief and temporary satiation by attempting to eject, via crying and physical distress, the unpleasant experience of wanting. The baby believes that it can magically feed itself via somatic distress.

Thus, for Freud, tolerance of frustration – or at least some mechanism to deal with the consequence of something we cannot do for ourselves – became the origin of primitive forms of thought. The distinction between hallucination as a magical way of avoiding reality and thinking as a way of adapting and coming to terms with external reality and its frustrations is crucial. Primitive forms of thought are based on an absence or lack of food or basic nurture. Optimally this is dealt with by beginning to think about that which is absent rather than merely experiencing a lack which cannot be understood. Freud's view was that the initial experience of feeding and being fed, in which frustration is both central and inevitable, is crucial to the development of thinking. As a way of dealing with frustration 'hallucinatory thought' may be inevitable and gratifying, but as a way of dealing with life and the external world sole reliance on this form of 'thought' could be deeply damaging since central to it is the denial of reality. Thinking must be associated with being in the world, and Freud's implication is that too much or too little frustration may lead us to a form of magical denial which impedes this process of adaptation.

In 'The importance of Symbol Formation in the Development of the Ego' (1930), Melanie Klein took this one step further by suggesting that there is a sophisticated capacity for primitive mental representation of somatic events or instinctual impulses, which she termed unconscious phantasy, from birth, which, if transformed into a more psychological form via symbolic representation, becomes the precursor of more mature thought. The Kleinian source of nourishment – the breast – is in phantasy split by the infant between the love and comfort it experiences when optimally fed, and a breast which, through its absence and the consequent frustration, is denigrated, if not actively hated. Klein believed that if this split, an inevitable and unavoidable consequence of the infant interacting with an environment at times both frustrating and satisfying, becomes too severe and too pernicious, then the capacity to symbolize is restricted, and mature thought is impossible. For Klein splitting is another way of denying reality – the recognition that the good and bad breast are one and the same – and an attack on mature thought.

For both Freud and Klein thinking is associated with adapting and coming to terms with reality; that is why thinking can be painful. The capacity to think, says Klein, is dependent on integrating splits. The infant needs to come to terms in manageable doses with an environment that is concurrently satisfying and frustrating. Only another can help him with that, which places thinking, as opposed to having thoughts, firmly in the context of relationships. Not being able to make up our minds assumes that our minds are made up of different parts that need integration. We may need others to help us with this.

Thinking together

Thinking is in essence an emotional experience of getting to know oneself and another, and for Klein the process for transforming emotional experiences into something which can be thought about is projective identification. Initially viewed as a defence whereby the infant splits off and projects unwanted or unpleasurable feelings or states into its mother or caretaker, Klein saw projective identification as the first mode of communication between the infant and its mother.

Through the projection of feelings and affective states into the mother – an implicit recognition that what we feel in the presence of another may influence and affect them – the infant communicates something which seeks understanding. It was Bion who thought about and described how something that was almost physiological in the infant was transformed into something more psychological by and with the mother. Bion suggested that if thinking is essentially an emotional experience, then the origins of coherent thoughts lie in our formative relationships. The development of thought cannot happen outside them. The infant will project feelings, perceptions, and sensations into another, usually the mother, which the mother contains and attempts to understand, that is think about. Through maternal thought a process of transformation is set in train: mothers thinking about their babies becomes the foundation of babies thinking about their mothers and the world around them. In this framework mothers who find it difficult to contain their baby's feelings, sensations or needs, will communicate this in some form (projective identification is a two-way process) and make the possibility of reciprocal thought a potentially dangerous activity for the infant. In educational settings a similar dynamic or process can be established between the student and individual tutors or the institution.

Bion distinguished between what he called 'beta elements' – sensory or somatic in nature – and alpha elements, more mental in character, and thus potentially able to be thought about. The interaction between mother and infant determines how and if beta elements are transformed into alpha ones. The value and importance of the transformation is underlined by Bion's suggestions that if beta elements remain unprocessed they might remain either in the body, as evidenced by psychosomatic or hypochondriacal symptoms – giving credence to the belief that thoughts originate in bodily experiences – or, since thought enables us to avoid precipitate action (we can think about what to do), unprocessed beta elements (sensations which have no scope for being changed into something more mental) are in danger of being impulsively acted upon.

In this sense beta elements are the raw material of possible creative thought which need to be harnessed by another person who has the capacity to transform them into alpha elements. Thus Bion's theory of thinking is essentially dialectical. An innate pre-conception (say the infant's innate expectation of the breast) meets a realization (the arrival of the breast or nurturing object) to produce a conception that offers the possibility of a mode of thought free from hallucinatory denial and consequently reality-based (thinking about a breast that both comes and goes and is only intermittently under your control). Thinking then is a way of both being recognized (someone is aware of our presence with its needs and demands), and of mastering frustration.

One of the implied consequences of this is that one has to have experienced frustration and acknowledged an absence for thinking to occur. Thought becomes a means by which frustration is tolerated. The ability to face frustration without hallucinatory denial becomes central to mature thinking. To evade frustration would be to deny reality and court an omnipotent grandiosity where an illusion of self-sufficiency leads to a delusion that we know everything and want for nothing. One cannot learn or think without some recognition of an absence in oneself. Small wonder that there are times when we would rather not think, and that such things as 'wasting time' or 'doodling' or the guilt associated with not working are potentially ways we avoid thought with its inevitable frustration. Thinking challenges our omnipotence. Doodling may be a way of holding an unconscious process, and represent an intermediary or transitory area where we experiment with or moderate what we can bear to think about. Resistance to thinking may be a way we accommodate to the limitations of one's own thoughts. If the perfect essay is unattainable, better to have thoughts rather than become a thinker, which would involve disillusionment and frustration. Realization – that is, thinking – always connotes a frustration.

The two processes which Bion described as aiding this transformation from thoughts to thinking are maternal reverie and containment. Reverie is that which the mother uses to transform the baby's projected sensations into tolerable feelings, while the ability to contain the infant's experience of pleasure or distress without any maternal imposition or infringement enables the infant to begin to make sense of its disjointed and fragmented world. Reverie is a 'state of mind that the infant requires of the mother' (Hinshelwood, 1989). Calm receptivity is required of the mother in order to 'take in the infant's own feelings and give them meaning':

> The idea is that the infant will, through projective identification, insert into the mother's mind a state of anxiety and terror which he is unable to make sense of and which is felt to be intolerable . . . Mother's reverie is a process of making some sense of it for the infant, a function known as 'alpha function'. Through introjection of a receptive, understanding mother the infant can begin to develop his own capacity for reflection on his own states of mind. When, for some reason, mother is incapable of this reverie for reflective meaning, the infant is unable to receive a sense of meaning from her; instead he experiences a sense of meaning having been stripped away, resulting in a terrifying sense of the

ghastly unknown [termed by Bion 'the nameless dread'].

Envy

The preoccupied mother or the excessively envious infant (in the sense of a need to destroy that which is perceived as good) will be a threat to the establishment of reverie. Bion implies that some infants find it impossible to tolerate the mother's capacity to contain experience which they themselves cannot, and that this provokes envious attacks. In this case excessive envy of the mother's capabilities would lead the infant to be unable to experience the mother's reverie as a relief. Through projection, the infant may experience the mother's reverie as an envious attack on the self, which would place maternal containment in the context of something that is potentially harmful and impoverishing. The problematic issue of envy forms the basis of what Bion terms 'attacks on linking', where anything which is felt to have the function of linking one object (person or thought) to another needs to be destroyed or negated. The resistance or inability to make links will obviously impede thinking. By not being able to link and think we avoid having to face connections between ideas or objects which we find painful or unacceptable, but at the cost of being unable to make sense of our experience. The need to keep things in bits and pieces, fragmented, to which thinking becomes a threat, provides a clue as to why joined up thought – and joined up writing – may be so problematic.

Containment

The mother who is able to tolerate and metabolize the baby's confusion and distress is the thoughtful mother who is able to return the baby's turmoil in a meaningful and non-threatening fashion. The infant develops the capacity to think by being able to assimilate the experience of thoughtful containment by the mother. Containment implies that one person temporarily holds a part of another before returning it in a transformed and benign form. An educational example of this would be of the student who, terrified of a book he does not understand, or is unable to digest, projects this into his tutor, who experiences the anxiety and is able to metabolize it in such a form that it can be 'returned' to the student in a less frightening form.

Should containment fail – or the infant experience a lack of recognition – he may go to greater lengths to achieve recognition, and in the absence of having his frustrations made comprehensible they are in danger of being stripped of meaning and impossible to think about. The infant needs the mother to make sense of its experience in a manner which is benign and safe, and free from excessive anxiety or uncertainty. In this way distress is detoxified by the mother and 'returned' to the infant. If the baby feels uncontained, then anxiety may increase, as does the infant's need to eject or expel sensations or feelings which are experienced as problematic or threatening. Thinking, and the ability to link mutually contradictory sensations or feelings – love and hate towards the same object, say – is then avoided. The infant who is not contained is in danger of continuing to resort to extreme splitting, and avoids having to make thoughtful connections about himself and the world around him. Splitting destroys the ability to think, throwing us back on earlier ways of dealing with the world, either through our bodies or impulsive action. Bion (1990) implies there is a fundamental difference between mature thinking, which has an integrative function in reconciling opposites or contradictions, and intelligence, where the ability to see and keep things separate may be an advantage. Thus some amount of denial – or splitting – in intellectual attainment may lead to quantum leaps in knowledge, although Bion does not elaborate on whether this has a personal cost.

The implication is that the mother or caretaker has to be able to tolerate the infant's frustration or distress without retribution or retaliation for mature thought to emerge. Initially it is the mother who thinks for the infant. Maternal thought aids the transformation of somatic sensations, of distress and desire, into symbolic forms. The infant will identify with a mother who is able to think for herself, and, initially at least, for the couple. Alternatively, the mother may be perceived by the infant as someone who profoundly misunderstands the nature of its self, or someone who through her curiosity steals something of value and so depletes the infant. This can lead to a disincentive to contemplate new experience or creative thought in order to avoid being misunderstood or stolen from. An intrusive aesthetic of mothering – as well as one which leads to fragmentation – may be experienced as a malign form of containment.

Learning and others

A distinction is drawn between 'non-thinking' ways of dealing with experience – rooted in somatic sensations and action – and thought itself, which, because it is potentially painful and problematic, is frequently avoided or attacked. Bion implies that coming to know what we feel and think involves surmounting obstacles which are not necessarily of our own making. Creative thought may depend in some measure on us learning from the emotional experience of attempting to know oneself via another. Thinking about others (understanding, remembering and noticing them) may help us think about ourselves.

This places our need for others as a foundation of learning and thinking. Learning about something is essentially learning about ourselves. Following Winnicott, the first experience of learning is in the reflection which we see in our mother's face (Winnicott, 1958). This gives us clues as to who we are and who we might become, and introduces us to the notion that we might learn about ourselves through the effect that our behaviour and affective state has on another. The first search, which lasts a lifetime, is the search for recognition of and by another. If it is a pleasure to hide, then it is a disaster not to be found, or even sought (Winnicott, 1965). For the self to be recognized as independent and different depends in no small measure on being recognized as similar by the other. If the other misunderstands me or denies me recognition, then my behaviour and experiences have no meaning and thought itself becomes perplexing. If thinking is the ability to think about similarities and differences – that is, external reality – then perverse thought is to deny differences. The yearning to remain in an undifferentiated world, where my thought becomes our thought, or vice versa, can lead to ways of knowing without thinking. Learning by rote or a predatory internalization of the tutor and the subject, may be a perverse, and unthinking, way of knowing.

Curiosity

If the ability to think, as opposed to having thoughts, is dependent to a large extent on our formative experiences, then what of curiosity? Like thoughts, are we born curious and only become disinterested as a result of our experience? If thinking is at times to be avoided, then can the same be said of curiosity?

We are surrounded by a profound ambivalence towards curiosity: not only did it kill the cat, but it is also frequently idle. The fate of Eve warns us what can happen if we dare to seek to explore our environment. Curiosity and creativity may be about experiencing and managing change; the ability to risk the suspension of one idea in the search for something new. Curiosity might involve tolerating uncertainty in not knowing the outcome of our search. We risk losing something familiar and known in the hope of discovering the new and as yet unknown. Curiosity also requires recognizing that something or someone is worth exploration. Curiosity is risky.

Psychoanalysis has frequently suspected a conspiracy between parents and teachers to extinguish curiosity from an early age. If, from its earliest days education demands of us submission and compliance, then how can a subversive curiosity be kept alive? If, as psychoanalysis suggested, early education, including parenting, is preoccupied with prohibitions, the child is left to choose between being compliant and good, or curious and naughty. As Anna Freud wrote (1955):

> Whoever has had the opportunity of being much with three- to four-year-old children, or of playing with them, is amazed at the wealth of their fantasy, the extent of their vision, the lucidity of their minds and the inflexible logic of their questions and conclusions. Yet the very same children, when of school age, appear to the adult in close contact with them rather silly, superficial and somewhat uninteresting. We ask with astonishment whatever has become of the child's shrewdness and originality! Psychoanalysis reveals to us that these gifts of the little child have not been able to hold their own against the demands which have been made upon him; after the expiration of his fifth year they are as good as vanished. Obviously to bring up 'good' children is not without its dangers. The repressions which are required to achieve this result . . . are paid for at a quite definite cost. The originality of the child, together with a great deal of his talents, are sacrificed to being 'good'. If the older children, compared to the little child, strike us as dull and inactive the impression is absolutely correct. The limitations which are placed on their thinking, and the obstacles put in the way of their original activities, result in dullness and incapacity to act.

Anna Freud implies that curiosity tends to be extinguished by parents and teachers – or schooling as an instrument of socialization – from an early age. In part this is because curiosity is initially a curiosity about the body which is defined as naughty:

> The universal aim of education is to make out of the child a grown up person who shall not be very different from the grown up world around him. Consequently we have the starting point for education. It regards as childlike behaviour everything in which the child differs from the adult . . . education struggles with the nature of the child, or – as the grown ups usually call it – his 'naughtiness'.

The problem is that we might need to be naughty in order to learn.

A 'guerrilla war' arises between the educators, however loosely defined, and child. Anna Freud goes on to suggest:

> Education wants to substitute for love of dirt a disgust of dirt, for shamelessness a feeling of shame, for cruelty sympathy, and in place of a rage for destructiveness a desire to cherish things. Curiosity and the desire to handle (that is, explore) one's own body

must be eliminated by prohibitions . . . step by step education aims at the exact opposite of the child's instinctive desires.

A conflict of interests exists between the child who 'seeks gratification of his own pleasures', and education which, 'proceeds as if the prevention of these objectives was its most important task'. How then can curiosity survive without excessive compliance or shame? Anna Freud suggests that we expect the child to have mastered his desires and conquered harmful and disturbing (for whom?) curiosity, by the time he arrives at school. If the earliest curiosity is about bodily functions, then it must be renounced, if necessary with the help of teachers and parents, as soon as possible. It is perhaps not surprising that 'formal' education has tended to begin at age five, when the intensity of the pre-pubertal years can be seen to be abating. The increasing tendency for formal education to begin earlier – nursery education if not playgroups – may suggest increasing desperation on our part to stifle any form of curiosity which can in any way be defined as 'naughtiness'. Parental anxiety about dealing with children's curiosity and its consequences, may lead to them sending children to others for the management of their 'curiosity'. The relative diminution of the child's instinctual conflicts during latency allows 'formal' learning to take place, but 'punishes most severely the child who (still) makes manifest his instinctual desires'.

While the most pernicious form of early education may be seen as 'shooting at sparrows with cannonballs', Anna Freud recognizes both the value and importance of the teacher and parent in nurturing a healthy curiosity, and the fact that it is not solely external forces which pose a threat to the child's ability to remain curious. In 1946 her father had already pointed to factors within the child, and the child's experience of its earliest relationships, as having a considerable bearing on the transformations undergone by infantile curiosity:

I have contributed nothing to the application of psychoanalysis to education, but it was understandable that the investigations of the sexual life of children, and of their psychological development, have attracted the attention of educationalists and have shown their task in a new light.

While knowledge, in its biblical usage, is essentially carnal, for Freud, curiosity about ourselves and others is intimately linked to the child's earliest curiosity about the distinction between the sexes. Childhood sexual curiosity might have something to teach us about our ability and capacity to be and remain interested in learning. The child needs to survive the recognition of anatomical difference if curiosity is not to be foreclosed. Freud suggests that the thirst for knowledge is initially directed at knowing about one's own or other bodies; the similarities and differences between the sexes and their link with the origin of children. If so, a primary curiosity about the body is converted through prohibitions, involving more often than not shame and disgust, into a curiosity of the mind. This, in some sense, is the origin of the psyche-soma split. Vestiges of earlier frames of mind persist not least in the search for, and acquisition of, a body of knowledge. Prohibitions, then, are fundamentally linked to what we allow ourselves (or are allowed) to be curious about.

Freud believed that the child's first researches were researches into the sexual life of the parents. Little Hans' curiosity made him ill (1909). Sex and knowledge go hand in hand:

> At about the same time that the sexual life of children reaches its first peak, between the ages of three and five, they also begin to show signs of the activity which may be ascribed to the instinct for knowledge or research ... we have learned that the instinct for knowledge in children is attracted unexpectedly early and intensely to sexual problems, and is in fact first possibly aroused by them (Freud, 1905).

If curiosity is about looking and finding out, what is it that we want to find out in childhood? For the infant the search for knowledge is associated with both finding out and an ability to entertain, and hold, contradictory thoughts. In the process of growing up, the answers to the questions we posed as children (e.g. what is the difference between the sexes, where do babies come from and how are they made) will determine how our curiosity survives the transition from erotic fantasies into creative pursuits. Parents' or educators' response to these initial questions will condition how comfortable we feel asking supplementary questions. If answered wrongly or brusquely we may be left feeling that the quest for knowledge is dangerous and to be avoided. If adults convey discomfort with this line of questioning or enquiry (or imply that it is shocking or frightening and best left secret), then this unease is in danger of becoming associated with any further exploratory curiosity or search for knowledge.

The Freudian child knows more than the lay adult dares to conceive: 'The fable of the stork is often told to an audience that receives it with deep, though mostly silent, mistrust.' This initial deception can lay the foundation for the child to believe adults will inevitably deceive it and leads to a form of explicit renunciation of curiosity, while implicitly nurturing a secret life where curiosity becomes a private preoccupation. For Freud, deception at this early stage leads the child to . . . refuse to believe the stork theory and from the time of this first deception and rebuff they nourish a distrust of adults and have a suspicion of there being something forbidden which is withheld from them by the grown ups, and . . . they subsequently hide their researches under a cloak of secrecy.

Freud appears to imply that this initial deception leads the child to be suspicious of both the adult and its own curiosity. A developmental side-effect, however, is that it may facilitate the child's increasing independence. Brooding and doubting on one's own forms the prototype of subsequent intellectual preoccupations towards the solution of problems. Conversely, sexual enlightenment may lead the child to experience its own curiosity as leading to a precocious loss of innocence. In finding out or learning, we may be submitting ourselves to a gradual process of disillusionment of childlike pleasures.

For Freud the child's curiosity in sexuality included what parents may do together. If the child perceives in its innocence the sexual act as involving violence, cruelty, and a domination and submission which it perceives as frightening, then its researches may have to be foreclosed or they become defined as dangerous and unthinkable. Curiosity becomes associated with erratic, unpredictable, and violent behaviour and fused with anxiety.

Curiosity and creativity

Freud believed that these early and impassioned experiences of fright, horror, and apprehension – initially towards sexual issues – can remain intensely arousing, and in later life be associated with aspects of curiosity, creativity, and educational accomplishment. Thus examinations and particularly demanding academic tasks may re-evoke the feelings associated with our earliest experiences of attempting to find out and its consequences. Infantile curiosity for Freud must become detached from its original object. If the child's initial search for knowledge is essentially (auto-) biographical – discovering secrets of a sexual nature about the function and origin of his own and other bodies – then development needs to aid the sublimation of the search from matters sexual to matters creative. Much depends on the nature (and more importantly the quality) of the interaction between the questioning child and the responding adult, and on the answers that are given to the child's initial questions. Where there are too many secrets it may be best not to know or attempt to find out.

Curiosity needs to emerge unscathed from its encounter with another.

As can be seen in our discussion of thinking, it follows that Melanie Klein, particularly in her writings about creativity, placed the child's experience of caretaking in the centre of the child's capacity to remain curious. Bion, too, sees the process between container and contained as being instrumental in the continued capacity to remain curious (1990):

> Projective identification makes it possible (for the infant) to investigate his own feelings in a person powerful enough to contain them. Denial of the use of this mechanism, either by the refusal by the mother to serve as the repository of the infant's feelings, or by the hatred and envy of the infant who cannot allow the mother to exercise this function, leads to the destruction of the link between infant and (mother) and consequently to a severe disorder of the impulse to be curious on which all thinking depends.

It is interesting in this context to note that Bion refers to curiosity as an impulse which would place curiosity as a physiological imperative awaiting recognition.

Splitting and projective mechanisms form the basis of early learning and are the derivative of curiosity. Curiosity for Klein is potentially destructive, while creativity is linked with reparation; what is repaired is the damage felt to be caused by the infant's envy aroused by its curiosity. It follows that while the Freudian infant's inhibition to its continued curiosity is potentially caused by the outcome of its researches, the Kleinian infant, immediately embroiled in an intense loving and hating relationship with its caretaker, is concerned about the damage it could cause, and seeks to make reparation. Thus for Klein it is not merely in relation to sexuality that curiosity is initially linked, but also to the infant's fantasies of envious destruction and retribution which need to be appeased. Unlike Freud, Klein saw the ability to be creatively curious as making something better, as a result of the infant's fears of damaging it. Creative curiosity becomes a way that creativity attempts to moderate or repair the damage that has potentially been done by curiosity. This may go some way to explaining why we are so ambivalent about curiosity: it is either turned into something else (a sublimation) or transformed into creativity, the function of which is to repair the damage done by destructive infantile curiosity.

If human behaviour is not solely about the satisfaction of instinctual impulses but also the search for meaningful contact and communication with others, curiosity, in its pre-sublimated and pre-reparative form, may be a way we communicate with and think about our environment. Thus growth and curiosity depend in part on what Winnicott has termed a 'facilitating environment', where the infant is recognized without being intruded upon and colonized by another. For Winnicott this area becomes a form of play, where through the interaction between self, other, and the transitional space created by the two, curiosity is able to flourish as opposed to being prematurely foreclosed. For Winnicott, the conditions which encourage curiosity include an experience of feeling real and recognized as of, but not part of, another without excessive compliance or impingement. Thinking, learning and curiosity may be impossible without this facilitating environment. Since the Winnicottian mother cares for her baby intuitively, without learning, a natural distinction is drawn between 'knowing' and 'learning', implying that learning and being taught should not deplete from an intuitive curiosity or understanding. Formal learning can involve a potential loss of intuitive curiosity: '[we need] to learn the things that can be taught . . . without the loss of what comes . . . naturally' (Winnicott, 1958). In this Winnicott appears at one with Jean Piaget, who is quoted as saying '. . . whenever you teach a child something you prevent him from inventing' (Bringuier, 1980). Thought and curiosity needs to be afforded a sanctuary from mindless learning.

Just as with thinking, where we can have thoughts alone but thinking requires others, we can be curious on our own, but curiosity demands our engagement with another. In this respect, curiosity challenges our narcissism; to be curious is to recognize another as something unfamiliar and different. If all we are interested in is sameness (or clinging to fantasies of self-sufficiency) then there is no need to summon our curiosity. In this sense curiosity may become a threat to the integrity of the self in that it involves an unpredictable encounter with another.

Curiosity may then be a state of mind that is evoked by and with the presence of another – another who represents something both new and uncertain. And it is to end or reduce this uncertainty that we engage in exploring the object of our curiosity. In the process of exploration we risk having to unlearn what we may know, in the hope of attaining mastery over the as yet unknown. Mastery, however, may involve acquiring superior knowledge, something which we feel we might want but less consciously be profoundly ambivalent about. We may be in danger of knowing too much and there may be questions that we prefer not to have answers to.

Taking risks with our curiosity depends on how hazardous we perceive the outside world to be. If the response to our childhood question 'why?' induces shame, guilt or humiliation, or courts disapproval, then it may not be worth risking being curious and we may retreat into a private and secret world, shunning curiosity, becoming the 'good' child who does not enquire further. A split is then in danger of developing between the 'good, obedient child' who is not curious and the 'bad or naughty child' who remains curious. Education is then faced with the difficulty of which child to encourage and reinforce. It may well be that the most formative experience in education is in learning something quite different from what has been taught; that is, as in the interaction between parent and child which produces something novel. The outcome of learning and being taught lies in producing something totally new, a synthesis of the relationship between teacher and taught, where a thoughtful curiosity is encouraged.

Learning as relating

Learning with the other is not learning from the other. It is the difference between internalizing a benign teacher and mindless incorporation. Clearly there are circumstances where it becomes impossible to learn from each other, and when reciprocal thinking is negated or destroyed. Christopher Bollas (1987) terms this form of 'learning' an 'extractive introjection' which involves 'an invasive attack on the other's mind, depleting the other and spuriously enriching the self'. Bollas quotes as an example of this an interaction between a student and teacher where the latter depletes the former of original thought, a process which leads to a confused and depleted student and a knowledgeable and spuriously enriched teacher. Learning and becoming educated may be more akin to a metamorphosis than becoming 'like' someone else. Just as both thoughts and curiosity need to undergo a transformation so it is in learning from another. In order to learn, our experience of another needs to be translated rather than incorporated. What we risk in the translation is the discovery of our own helplessness. In thinking we always face the unknown and unfamiliar, yet need to ensure we avoid the danger of making it prematurely known. Learning is like a relationship because it starts with the recognition of a lack, is painful, and we may yearn for simple expedient solutions which will precociously fill up the imagined deficit. If we were self-sufficient we would not have to learn. Insecurity, fear of failure, our own narcissism may all contribute to our ambivalence towards learning, just as, because it is infinite and by definition confronts us with doubt and uncertainty, we may balk at knowledge itself. Knowledge knows no boundaries, which can be frightening.

Ambivalence about our need for others ensures that we are always ambivalent about thinking, curiosity, and learning, since all require another. We may go to great lengths to avoid recognizing that we need others to think, remain curious and learn. The need for independence conflicts with the need to be recognized and valued, which can only come from another. We are ambivalent about having to acknowledge that without others there is no creative thought, which may explain why it is that in higher education thinking is widely seen as a solipsistic and solely cerebral activity. As we have seen, thinking and knowing can be painful; we all wish to avoid certain forms of insight. If we accept that thinking takes place within a relationship, then 'independent thought' brings up issues of separation, while 'differences of opinion' brings up the possibility of conflict between ourselves and others.

As Popper (1972) said, the child's mind is less a bucket into which things are poured than a searchlight where the child actively scours its environment for things which may be of interest. Unless it succeeds in finding another and being recognized, thinking, learning, and curiosity may be impossible. Learning, mediated as it is between the teacher, knowledge, and the student, is in essence a transitional experience, an area of illusion where difference and similarities can be explored. If the 'capacity to be alone' – a result of being allowed to be alone in the presence of someone else, i.e. mother – is fundamental to development, then to be able to think and study on one's own can only occur as a result of having been able to be curious about, and think with, another.

Thought and curiosity involve change, and in the next chapter I shall look at some of the inevitable transitions which the student faces in higher education. These transitions may confront us with the question of whether we want education to transform us into something, or someone, different?

4
Transformations

[it is to] escape from the whole unfair business of having to have a whole verifiable history, that [we] leave home to go to college . . . without giving it much thought at all, we consecrate the world with our own subjectivity, investing, people, places, things and events with a kind of idiomatic significance . . . the objects of our world are potential forms of transformation (Christopher Bollas, 1987).

Winnicott (1958) suggests that the infant is in transition from being merged with the mother to being separate. Similarly, the process of becoming a student will involve a succession of transitions, and the potential for any number of transformations. In the transition between home and college, the possibility exists of becoming something, or someone, else. There is a certain inevitability about the wish to become (an) other which is reinforced by the combined pressure of higher education and the developmental imperative to grow up.

Transitional objects

For Winnicott, transitional objects represent the first intermediate area of experience between the mother or caretaker, the self, and the world. Transitional objects originate in thumb- and fist-sucking in infancy, through to the use of soft toys and early play, and include both objects and people. These objects can come to represent something outside yet essentially of the self, the first 'not-me' experience which is subjectively created. As an intermediary area created by, but not of, the self they have the potential to become the basis of illusion. It is in our power to create something out of that which may be objectively seen as nothing. For Winnicott, transitional objects form the basis of other illusory experiences, such as creativity, art, religion, and learning:

> This intermediate area of experience, unchallenged in respect of its belonging to inner or external (shared) reality, constitutes the greater part of the infant's experience and throughout life is retained in the intense experiencing that belongs to the arts and to religion and to imaginative living, and to creative . . . work (1953).

This transition, involving the move from absolute dependence, through a kind of magical omnipotence, towards relative independence, involves a journey towards the recognition of an objectivity which constitutes the basis of both scientific method and intellectual pursuits. This includes the increasing capacity for symbolization and reality testing, which create the building-blocks for learning. Note, however, the danger of becoming too objective, as Winnicott (1950) said: 'those who are most reliably objective are often comparatively out of touch with their own inner world's richness'. In this sense the transitional object can facilitate a balanced integration. We are never really, despite attempts to delude ourselves, either fused with our mothers (totally subjective and in ignorance of a world apart) or separate (and capable of a spurious objectivity). The capacity to use symbol and metaphor in an 'as-if' way is fundamental to most if not all educational ventures. The child's use of this first transitional object is the forerunner of the person's ability to engage with others in cultural and intellectual discourse. This would lend support to the view that learning, intellectual curiosity and cultural interests, are developmental achievements rather than displaced instinctual desires.

In the Winnicottian world, it is a function of the mother to nurture the infant's illusion in order to facilitate the infant's omnipotence and also its sense of innate self-worth and potential. The infant needs to believe everything is possible prior to the recognition that some things may not be. 'Illusion', says Phillips (1988) 'was initially the infant's belief that he had created what in fact he had found'; before the humbling recognition that someone had been there to help him. Thus, says Winnicott, '. . . the mother's eventual task is gradually to disillusion the infant, but she has no hope of success unless at first she has been able to give sufficient opportunity for illusion'.

Education, like our earliest relationships, may need to respect the student's anticipatory desire to believe and nurture the illusion which education, or becoming educated, may offer. We need to think that we have discovered something ourselves before acknowledging that we have been taught. The art is to help us to believe that, not having learnt solely by ourselves (or at least having been able to do it with the at times unintrusive assistance of another) is not too devastating or humiliating. The sudden awareness that we have been mothered or taught, while all the time believing we have done it ourselves, is not merely crushing but the precursor of a particularly virulent form of resentment.

Education beckons as an illusion, but the danger exists that its rewards may be illusory:

John, a 21-year-old graduate student, was becoming increasingly concerned about what he referred to as a 'mental block', which prevented him from concentrating and working effectively. Consequently, it had the effect of causing considerable anxiety as he had always previously been able to work successfully. He believed that there must be an academic or 'technical' solution to this which could magically transform him and enable him to continue with his studies in the familiar successful fashion.

He was a somewhat driven and ambitious young man, who had planned out his academic and subsequent career in meticulous detail, to the extent of knowing what he would be doing at what age for the foreseeable future. It came as a shock to him to be informed upon his arrival at the university at the beginning of the academic year that he would not be able to enrol in the course of his choosing, but first would have to successfully complete a year studying a subject not to his liking, and one that would not fit into his career plans. Eventually, he appeared passively and despondently to accept this requirement (despite at some level being enraged), but it led to a persistent feeling of being on trial and excluded, or in some way, unacceptable to the institution and himself. Feelings of being an outsider were reinforced by the fact that he lacked any academic peer group. It was clear that the whole situation was extremely galling, as it challenged both his ambition and his hopes for the future.

This account was given in a frenzied, tense fashion, his speech and body stiff with despairing outrage. However, when talking about his background, the 'non-academic part' of him, he relaxed and the story became more alive and vibrant, despite being viewed by John as of little import, given his academic problems.

He came, shamefully as he saw it, from very humble origins. His father was a lorry driver and it was important that John became something else; not merely different, but more successful. Something that would invest him with the status and prestige that he felt his background denied him. As a consequence it came as no surprise to discover that he wanted to join the diplomatic service. The problem was that from an early age it appeared that education evoked feelings of being either on trial or an outsider, involving as it did a certain form of estrangement from his origins. The belief that education could transform him into something else was palpable.

His mother had died when he was 13, and, partly out of a wish on his family's behalf to 'better himself', he was sent to live with a well-to-do aunt, where he felt out of place and under pressure to fit in with her expectations. Both his late mother's and aunt's desires (for whom?) were experienced as forms of impingements and did not allow scope for his own hopes or illusions; survival and compliance appeared the only options. As a result he became quiet, reserved, academic and driven to successfully become someone else, without the capacity to 'use' either others or the transitional space which education could potentially offer. Illusion, and the more valuable capacity for disillusionment (that is, knowing what we want in the context of what might be possible) had been unavailable for him. It was in some ways not surprising that the academic issues that had resulted in this 'mental block' were not dissimilar (in fact, ran in parallel) to his personal and familial history. His desperation to fit it, both with his aunt's and the university's demands, at considerable cost to his personal integrity and self-esteem; his pervasive feelings of being an outsider or on trial from his family of origin, aunt and university, and his belief that his work needed to be of a high order, if not perfect, in order to attain the transformation he was seeking, reflected his sole method of gaining positive approval as a child. Seen in this light, his 'mental block' could be viewed as an opportunity to question the transformation he was so desperately seeking.

John poses the question: What transition is higher education in fantasy expediting? Is one of the goals a metamorphosis of the self? If education has the capacity to function as a form of psychological and social transformation, how can this come about? Education may evoke, and be a repetition of, a previous experience when our hopes, fears, expectations, and sense of self, have had the potential of being transformed by another. As babies we may look hopefully towards another to convey both meaning and being. The mother, as the infant's 'other self', has the capacity and potential to transform the baby's internal and external environment. The infant in its dependence relies on the mother for sustaining '. . . the baby's life and transmits to the infant, through her own particular idiom of mothering, an aesthetic of being that becomes a feature of the infant's self' (Bollas, 1987).

The mother, then, is experienced less as a distinct object or person, and more as a process of transformation. Mothering or being mothered is an invitation to become someone (else).

If our mothers initially transform us into what we are or could become they become linked with a specific process that can alter our experience of ourselves. They become co-conspirators in a project to metamorphose the self. Bollas contends that this develops as a result of the infant's experience of the mother as a process of alteration. The fundamental quality here is that it is primarily an experience of mothering as a process, rather than 'knowing' a mother who is separate and has discreet functions. For Bollas (1987), '. . . the experience of the object precedes knowing the object.' It is not the person so much as the process that is internalized by the infant. As a result we may remain particularly susceptible to seeking out and using any object or process which has the capacity to function in a similar fashion. This initial experience in infancy of a transformational process may leave us continuously searching in later life for a similar experience which repeats this process. In adulthood this search would comprise a certain unconscious yearning for or anticipatory disposition towards a repetition of this earliest experience. It is thus at some level 'known', but with no capacity to conceptualize the experience in words or thought, 'unthought'. As Bollas says, '. . . transformational object seeking is an endless memorial search for something in the future that resides in the past . . .' Consequently, the process embodies concurrent hope and disappointment.

The way this comes about has certain similarities, but also significant differences, in both method and function with the mother's ability to contain the infant's demands and desires, be they anger or hunger, which are transformed via the mother's sensitivity to her infant's needs into contentment and satiation. We may look hopefully towards the transformational object as potentially transforming us into something we would like to be, or alternatively we may need to protect ourselves against a transformational object that could be experienced as inherently intrusive and demanding.

Where the interaction between mother and infant lacks synchronicity and reciprocity based upon the recognition of the other's needs, and the relationship is based primarily on one partner's narcissistic needs, the possibility arises that we may fear what we might be made into; something different in the service of another. Where mothering is experienced predominantly as an impingement, we may dislike or resist via excessive compliance or the construction of a secret self what we are being turned into or invited to become. The intrusive experience of this form of transformational process would then predispose us to being fearful of either domination or exploitation. However, it may also be welcomed as known and safe, albeit at some cost to our personal integrity. The search for the transformational object may then involve a compulsive quest to repeat a process which inhibits thinking for oneself, or experiencing oneself as real, and avoids the creative use of being transiently dependent on another in the service of our own development. Learning something new from another then becomes a problem.

Alternatively, following Winnicott, if the baby has not been 'de-illusioned' in the service of gradually introducing the world to the infant in manageable doses, a variation of this process in education would be the development of an omnipotent grandiosity, where the search for perfection in intellectual or academic excellence can be seen as an attempt to repair an earlier deficit. It is interesting to note the importance ascribed by Bollas (1987) to language in this process. The mother transforms the '. . infant's sense and gesture into language for she continuously comments on the baby in the baby's presence. As she comments on the baby's gesture, she also frequently alters the baby's environment in his favour, thus linking language with the actual transformation of the environment. Speaking then becomes associated with the actual transformation of the self and partially compensates for the narcissistic losses implicit in the necessity to speak to the other about the self.' Believing, as did Freud (1917) that this process of transformation (involving as it does the 'object casting its shadow over the subject') takes place when the infant has neither mental representation nor language, the child is left knowing something of the attributes of what has affected him without the capacity to talk or think about it. Language, when it arrives, becomes the medium to explore that which is both experienced and known, but not yet thought. Learning may then help us to think about what we already 'know', but only dimly perceive – the 'unthought known'.

Education as transformation

Education can become an accomplice, willingly or not, in this process. The result is frequently a wish for a process that will transform how we experience ourselves, or alternatively how we are viewed by others. What is frequently seen in education is a hope that by transforming the latter via superior knowledge or qualifications, the former will be 'cured'. Education then becomes sought for its transformative function, rather than any of its intrinsic qualities, such as the search for and pleasure in knowledge. In this case learning and knowledge are merely seen as a means to an end. Education becomes a form of 'anticipatory daydream' about the self, involving the denial or neglect of current reality and the absence of any curiosity, doubt, and sense of exploration about what is being learnt. Education as a medium for altering the self ceases to be an object of desire (something that we want and are willing to suffer for), but something that we need, to use more or less ruthlessly in pursuit of personal transformation.

For Bollas, the anticipation of being transformed by an object (say, education) can lead to an attitude of veneration towards it, so that even though the transformation may disappoint, the object may still be 'sacredly over-valued'. The alternative, because it is only valued for its utilitarian qualities, may be that the object is secretly denigrated. In this context, it is interesting to note how frequently the most vehement critics of non-vocational education come from those in society that have been most 'highly' and prestigiously educated. An impressive C.V. does not always correlate with either being or feeling impressive. The transformation may disappoint. As we saw in the case of John, the need to find something in the future to transform both the present and past may involve a certain form of illusory self-deception, and the deferment of a perceived gratification to some unspecified time in the future when one is fully qualified or complete. In this sense 'the qualification' becomes a desperate search for a form of psychic health or integration. It can remedy something that is experienced as incomplete, integrate something that feels fragile, repair a 'basic fault' or compensate for a perceived lack in the personality.

If we need to be held and healed by our mothers, then the same may be true of education. Education offers fantasies of repetition or renewal containing wishes to remodel the past, escape from the past, or to remain identified with the past. The difficulty for those who view education in these terms is that rather than becoming another, we may finally be left encountering our old selves, which we had hoped we had, chameleon-like, left far behind. The old self we are reunited with or cannot shed may well be, as Bollas says, 'an identification with parental or familial figures' from whom separation or escape has proved problematic.

The dilemma then becomes, do we really know who we want to be (come), or is it a surprise finding out? Deterministically knowing who or what we want to become poses certain problems. In being parented or taught, the mechanisms of our transformation may fail to collude with our aspirations, and gently or ruthlessly need to de-illusion us. Just as mothers have the capacity to transform the world for their babies, babies can potentially have a similar function for their mothers. Transformations are, in essence, reciprocal possibilities:

> [the] infant requires separation and disillusionment from the transformational mother, but mother must also suffer a let down brought about by the real needs of the infant, which mitigates the mother's unconscious wish for an infant to be her transformational object (Bollas, 1987).

The inappropriate use of a student by a tutor as a transformational object is not unknown. Tutors who are desperate for their tutees to become different or similar versions of themselves, or who have difficulty recognizing the student's autonomy and independence, may be making up for a narcissistic deficit in themselves or using the student to effect a personal transformation. This involves the refusal to recognize the student as both different and real, since successful transformations depend upon the recognition of the other as unique and separate.

Some vulnerable students, doubting their own competence and lacking sufficient trust in the 'benign disposition' of their tutors or educational institutions, may seek out failure as a way of confirming the 'static nature of their earlier transformational experience'. Bollas suggests that the inability to use the transformational object (or its absence) may result in the seeking out and adhesive attachment to an object which makes change impossible. The student who doggedly enrols on a course, or repeatedly re-sits examinations knowing at some level that success is illusory, is by seeking a 'negative transformation' in effect recreating an earlier pathological situation. Some students expect education to confirm their worst fears about themselves.

The graduate student

While education has to offer developmental hope, it needs at the same time to be freed from any illusory or idealized function. Education may deliver a transformation, but the essence of learning is the surprise in the discovery that it does. As we have seen with the example of John, there are psychological dangers in complying to an object solely for its transformational potential, not least because we cannot allow ourselves to be surprised by what we are discovering. Curiosity is beset with risk, as it may threaten the very transformation we think we need or desire. If becoming a student involves not merely a transition, but also the prospect of a personal transformation, then there may be certain times during a student's career when they are more susceptible or vulnerable to this process. One of these times may occur when we decide to become graduate students:

Nick had embarked on a doctorate course immediately after completing an undergraduate degree with distinction. He looked forward to the course, methods of study, the graduate life, and status with considerable pleasure, having as an undergraduate secretly envied graduates for their appearance of wisdom and freedom from what he saw as the petty restrictions of undergraduate life. Assuming that becoming a graduate would lead to his becoming the man he had always wanted to be, he quickly found a research topic and arranged accommodation in a bedsit in a distant part of the town.

Nick was the only child of rather severe parents who separated when Nick was 11. Nick remained with his father, with whom he developed an intense relationship fraught with tensions and misunderstandings. He was sent to a formal, structured school and led a highly organized life, which continued as an undergraduate. He enjoyed the sociable experience of learning which seminars provided, and the manifold social events that were laid on for undergraduates. An additional benefit was that by having a series of tutors for different topics, Nick avoided the necessity of making too intense relationships with any one tutor which would carry with it the danger of replicating his uneasy relationship with his father. However, he still felt that he had 'something to prove'; somehow graduates appeared more autonomous, worldly, and independent.

Socially Nick had never had a girlfriend, but had always enjoyed and vigorously entered into the gregarious and communal lifestyle of other undergraduates, where through both his academic ability and his tendency to shine, via his wit and enthusiasm fed by his friends' positive approbation, he became a well-liked member of the group. Academically he enjoyed working to deadlines, and valued the regular feedback his essays provoked, particularly if, as frequently happened, the feedback was fulsome in its praise.

Within six months of starting his doctorate, Nick was admitted into hospital suffering from a depressive breakdown.

Becoming a graduate may involve a particular form of transition, made more problematic by the appearance of it being more of the same; by appearing a seamless transition, the experience of becoming a graduate student may lull us into a specific form of complacency. Graduate students are immediately faced with a plethora of difference after the often half-conscious expectation of encountering something familiar and similar. One of the major differences is that most institutes of higher education are predominantly undergraduate institutions, where the twin demands of teaching and research may lead to graduates being peripheral to the central task. Despite the often large numbers of graduate students, in many universities they form the base of the iceberg; unseen yet relied upon to ensure the tip is visible. (As Nick at one point said to me when referring to graduate students, 'We are the sponge beneath the icing.')

The transition to graduate life may be particularly disruptive as a result of the relative lack of structure in comparison to life as an undergraduate. Graduates may require a greater degree of self-motivation, particularly in a framework where academic teaching and deadlines are more diffuse. The nature of the task may be unclear, and consequently confusing and daunting, which can be reinforced by the lack of explicit deadlines and the relatively infrequent supervisory meetings or formal teaching. It becomes difficult for a graduate student to maintain the same relationship to academic work which they had as an undergraduate. The task becomes invested with a particular significance, often associated with some deeply personal transformational function, where the perceived lack of feedback or structure is in danger of being viewed as a very specific and personal form of persecution.

The need for self-motivation is paramount, as motivation no longer necessarily comes from any external source, be they tutors, peers, or family. This can induce a form of solipsistic apathy or despair, made more intense by the belief that while the student does not always choose to become an undergraduate, the decision to become a graduate student is generally one of personal choice. The balance between work and leisure, always potentially difficult for a student, assumes greater significance for graduates as there are unlikely to be structures which indicate a clear demarcation between the two. The solitary nature of the task adds to the difficulty of finding any points of comparison or support against which one can objectively measure oneself. The lack of a formal framework may increase self-reproach. These reproaches may differ along subject lines. Scientists may believe they need to be in the laboratory all the time, with associated feelings of guilt and peer-group disapproval if they are not, while graduate students in the humanities may well need to reinvent the working day and establish a work and social schedule which suits them individually.

Graduate study, in particular for higher degrees which involve research, can be very lonely, and may come as a shock to those students used to and expecting the more sociable and communal undergraduate life. For these students it may be the first time that the reality of what an academic life involves is faced. This is likely to be a major de-stabilizing factor, particularly for those students who as undergraduates did not anticipate or spend some time contemplating what the implications of this transition might involve. These students may have to mourn the glory that was their undergraduate selves before being able to actively engage with their graduate lives.

Study for a research degree with one supervisor clearly offers the opportunity for various forms of attachment. A major facet of the graduate experience is to be solely dependent, possibly for the next two to four years, on one person's approbation, approval, nurture, and interest. The quality of the relationship that is established with the supervisor is possibly the single most important factor in the life of a graduate student. At undergraduate level the student will have had a range of subject tutors offering the possibility both of escape (if you do not get on with one, there are always others in the future with whom you might) and the ability to regulate the intensity of the tutorial relationship. Undergraduate teaching is generally done in small or moderately sized groups, which has the effect of de-fusing the nature of possible relationships which could be established between teacher and taught, and limiting the possibilities of a particularly intense transference (or transformational process) from being enacted. The supervisory relationship at graduate level does not offer this protection; the particular intensity, value and importance ascribed to this relationship offers an invitation for it to assume a significance well beyond the purely academic. More so than at undergraduate level, it becomes invested with and comes to represent something symbolic rather than something which is real or actual. A particularly intense form of transformational process may be unwittingly encouraged, which may detract, not merely from the academic task, but also from one's own development. The aspirational element of the transformational process may be an invitation to anxiety and self-doubt:

Ethel, a 25-year-old graduate student, had returned to full-time education after a period spent working in industry. She had always secretly seen herself as scholarly, and despite considerable parental opposition and self-doubt, she eagerly embarked on the task of becoming an academic.

She was the youngest child of elderly, non-academic parents, and had been plagued throughout her life by doubts as to whether she was able or had permission to take risks, which an academic career would, according to her parents, involve. Her parents were both cautious, suspicious of 'getting ideas above one's station', and prone to depression. She had struggled throughout her under-graduate career with these issues, and had managed to achieve a brittle sense of independence from the family culture and expecta-tions when working in 'a proper job' and living in a flat of her own. However, she had always secretly nurtured a desire to escape from the constraints of the family's expectations and become someone different. This would involve engaging in something which would confirm and prove once and for all her separateness. She needed to believe and have evidence to prove that the past was another country.

However, when embarking on her chosen course, she found herself plagued by an inability to work or to engage in graduate social activities, consumed as she was with self-doubt and depres-sion. She found herself worrying about her parents – their physical health and whether she would ever see them again, since she was studying at a university a considerable distance from her home town. She spent most of her time ruminating in a state of depressive agitation about her capability for her course, whether she should allow herself a social life, and tormented by a pervasive feeling of impending disaster.

Having established a form of parentally approved independence in her previous job, she now found herself faced with the possible consequences of daring to wish to be different. She was going to be punished for wanting and seeking a personal transformation. Her depression helped maintain a tenuous link with home. Separation and the wish for a personal transformation which would challenge, if not destroy, the values of her family were dealt with by effectively becoming stuck; she could not betray her family by seemingly having a good time and enjoying her studies. Ethel remained identified with them in a form of depressive hopelessness. If she was not continuously worrying about her parents she might not think about them at all; in the struggle to become a scholar (a personal transformation) the past just would not be jettisoned. Never having been able to risk becoming different courted a sense of fraudulance, and Ethel became excessively dependent on her elusive supervisor's approval, frequently disturbed by a belief that he shared in the familial assumption that she had overreached herself. Attempts to transform the self were to be met with either failure or punishment. She would find herself meticulously analysing the 'subtext' of the infrequent discussions with her supervisor for any evidence that his praise meant the opposite or that his 'constructive criticisms' confirmed her self doubt and hubris. Entertaining 'ideas above your station' was dangerous.

Interestingly, Ethel was troubled about having to do research. While she had no difficulty in constructing essays from textbooks, she was daunted and intimidated by the demand to seek out the original texts, discover new manuscripts, and produce something original. For her, the psychological aspect of research was not to piece things together, leading to integration, but to court the risk of separation and fragmentation.

It may be helpful to ask, what individual script is involved in becoming a graduate student? – what issue is the act of becoming a graduate student meant to resolve? Graduate studies, because of their more explicitly functional or vocational nature, are more likely to be associated with some transformational project than undergraduate studies. However, as first degrees increasingly become viewed in more vocational terms, undergraduate studies will become more explicitly fused with transformational aspirations. Vocational courses differ in psychological substance not least by the fact that students on specifically vocational courses have a different relationship to their own curiosity. Finding out is potentially less important than knowing and becoming. The bored and resigned medical student who said, 'I know it all, it's just a question of learning it by heart', was merely expressing a simple psychological truth. Hearts, however, tend to have difficulty with rote learning. Learning by rote leads to a loss of intuition. This student was willing to suffer five years of tedium and ritual humiliation (not infrequently associated with vocational, particularly medical, courses) in the anticipation of becoming what he always knew he wanted to be, and to be able to be the instigator of the humiliations rather than their recipient. It is interesting to note just how many vocational courses include an almost ritualistic element of denigration or humiliation in the structure of their courses. This has the effect of reinforcing an almost pervasively unconscious cycle whereby what we passively are forced to endure as students we subsequently – when we are suitably 'qualified' – actively enforce on others. The masochist can be a sadist *manqué*. Knowing what we want to be in advance is a foreclosure of life.

One interesting facet of graduate study, often associated with the transformational project, is the choice of research interest which the student may make. This may reveal a thinly disguised psychological script. The student whose father was a doctor, chose as his thesis topic patient care in general practice, but changed after a few months to study the effect of nursery provision on the under-fives, his mother having returned to work when he was very young. He was attempting to explore where his most profound frustrations really lay. Research may involve exploring our own histories.

We may wish for a transformation or merely aim for a form of emulation, where the wish to become like someone else takes precedence over any attempt to become oneself. We are then condemned to pursue our academic studies without having a comfortable perception of ourselves, merely aspiring to be like someone else. This would be a wish for a form of identification that denies difference, and where the transformational process goes into reverse; the object being to stay the same.

The mature student

To talk of a mature student may appear a contradiction in terms. It would imply that there is also something called an 'immature student' from whom the mature student differs in having a more 'adult' approach to his studies. However, as we have seen, while the immature may use education to stay the same, this can never be the case for the mature student. By definition the mature student is actively seeking a positive transformation. For the mature student, studying is never more of the same to put off the evil day when some form of change is unavoidable, but an active engagement with something new, which, in a paradoxical way, reminds us of something familiar in our pasts. Mature students have all at some time in their lives been immature pupils. It is the relationship to previous educational experiences that conditions the mature student's transformational script.

Mature students share with their younger counterparts the mixture of expectation and helplessness when confronted by higher education, often, however, with the added ingredient of having failed in their previous encounters with formal education. A second chance is offered to those who, perhaps for social or psychological reasons, failed to take full advantage of educational opportunities in their youth. As we have seen, one of the consequences of having to make formative educational and vocational decisions at a very young age is that they are often made for the wrong reasons. Reparation, repair, repetition, and retribution become the leitmotifs of the mature student. For the mature student, the transformational script may include the sense of possibility; scripts are not written in advance, nor are they liable to be written by others.

One of the difficulties for both the mature student and their institutions is whether to recognize the notion of difference. Often a collusive silence is in evidence. If mature and traditional students are really the same, then students can continue to be treated as a homogeneous group, without any need to tease out and act upon specific distinctions. In this field, as in others, differences may be understated or denied because of a fear that once acknowledged they may be deemed judgemental or evaluative. Difference for the mature student might imply inferiority. The fear of inferiority is central to the ambivalence that mature students have towards their peers, learning, and their educational institutions. Fantasies of inferiority, rooted in previous failures, lead the mature student to wish to be treated in the same way as the traditional student, while at the same time to yearn for some understanding and acknowledgement of the nature of their difference.

Developmental confusion and adolescent ambivalence are less likely to become educational obstacles for mature students, making transformational projects more attainable. In adolescence, as we have seen, learning may need to take second place to the task of growing up, and it is not always clear why we are studying. The mature student, however, is rarely in any doubt about why they are studying, not least because the sacrifices are often both great and self-evident. Motivation therefore is less likely to be a psychological obstacle, since for the mature student motivation usually has to do with change (a positive transformational wish), while for younger students, unconscious motivation may be about fantasies of homeostasis, which will function to prevent change.

Motivation by itself, however, is rarely able to combat the pervasive sense of inferiority experienced by many mature students. The feeling of inferiority can also be reinforced by a culturally sanctioned sense of abnormality. In a society that sees education or being educated as something which happens at or by a certain age, and deems those that have left school at 16 as having failed academically, the mature student is in danger of being viewed as both a failure and abnormal. While the former can be addressed by a return to study, the latter becomes a central part of the mature student's experience. Abnormality and inferiority thus may become internalized.

The project associated with returning to education is for mature students as diverse as for their traditional contemporaries. While there are similarities, it is the differences which are significantly interesting. The mature student will embrace change, or at least the notion of change, in a way which may be abhorrent for the younger student. Thus education becomes a developmental progression, rather than a wish to stay the same or to stop the clock. While the mature student may share the notion of education as a solution to a personal, vocational, or social problem, it is much more likely that education is seen as an opportunity to correct a previously experienced wrong or failure. The pupil who disliked school and may have been rejected by education, or whose family harboured an ambivalent attitude to education, will be the mature student with a mission, and something to prove. Success can punish or prove something to those that expected little of us. In that sense, the successful mature student may be making themselves known to others – parents or teachers perhaps – in a way that is impossible for the adolescent student, who has a different relationship to his own success.

A contemporary disaffection with one's life, vocational or personal, may lead to an existential crisis for which becoming a mature student may be a perceived solution. The role of wife or mother may be transformed by education. In 'Educating Rita', it is not only Rita who is being educated. We may be seeking to educate others in our true natures while subtly fearing or hoping estrangement or rescue from our current life and relationships.

Mature students may also believe that knowledge, or a formal qualification, will serve to substantiate strongly held views derived from lengthy life experiences, and wish to prove themselves in an area previously experienced as unattainable. The mature student may well have struggled with an ambivalent attitude to their own competitiveness, which resulted in under-functioning or failure at an earlier stage of their education, which now has the opportunity to be reworked. Returning to education can lead to a specific form of over-compensation: mature students, since they are older, may believe they have to be better and wiser than the traditional student. It can be humiliating and shameful not to know at an age when one should. The mature student's transference to 18 year olds may be either to a younger sibling, their own children, or a younger version of themselves. A consequence of this may be a specific form of transference which may provoke a severe obstacle to the mature student's ability to study successfully. It may not always be pleasant or constructive to be confronted later in life with aspects of ourselves when we were 18. Feeling inferior to an 18 year old who could be your son or daughter may evoke envy as well as issues associated with missed opportunities. Being taught by someone younger than you who knows more may produce a peculiar form of transference. A change of role and an academic environment may re-activate issues which were avoided at 16. What we thought we had safely left behind when leaving school, often involving running away from something represented by education, may return to haunt us at a time in our lives when we are singularly unprepared for it.

Mature students will by definition have a different relationship to failure and success than their successful 18-year-old contemporaries, whose experience of failure has at most been transient. For the mature student, failure and education are likely to be synonymous. While when younger we can believe that it has been others or circumstances that have conspired to prevent us succeeding, as mature students success or failure is ours and ours alone. Failure is the mature student's trusted if despised companion, in a way unimaginable for the successful adolescent student. The mature student, while expecting the worst, may well find that the best – success – is equally problematic. Transformations can succeed in one area of our lives while simultaneously and surprisingly disappoint in another:

Jean was a 39-year-old mother of two children, who, wishing to become a solicitor, returned to university to read law. Reading law would right the perceived wrongs of her childhood when, because of a stormy and turbulent family background, Jean had been preoccupied with a developmental rebellion, which had led her to leave school early and drift into a succession of poorly paid jobs in the service industries.

She came from a large family and had lived in a tiny secluded community in the Scottish Highlands. Her mother, whose own father had been a crofter eking out an impoverished existence, had decided when Jean was 15 to 'better herself', and began to train as a teacher, leaving the children to 'fend for themselves', her studies making her unavailable to the children for long periods. Jean had, after a succession of unsatisfactory love affairs, married, in her late 20s, a man who was considerably older than herself. She 'bore him' two children and dutifully followed him around the country when his frequent changes of jobs required the family to move. Becoming increasingly aware of a need to 'better herself' (although not of the link with the maternal precedent), she enrolled in a course at a university a considerable distance from the family home. Her husband, his ambivalence about Jean's course of action showing, refused to accompany her, so Jean and the children moved away. Seeing her husband at weekends, because of the academic demands on her time, became less frequent. This coincided with an increasing recognition on Jean's part of another life from which her husband was effectively excluded, and in comparison to which he appeared both dull and limited.

Jean struggled with the twin demands of looking after the family and a return to an academic life which was both unfamiliar and alien, if exciting, functioning as it did to remind her of the reasons for her previous academic failure. Increasingly becoming aware of her dissatisfaction with her marriage, she began to move towards formalizing the separation, and initiated divorce proceedings against her by now estranged husband. Becoming daily more aware of her own capabilities and aspirations, the reasons for marrying her husband began to remind her of an earlier life which she now wanted both to transcend and forget. Painful though it was she divorced her husband, but from the day of the decree nisi she found she was unable to think clearly, as a consequence of which she was unable to write any essays, or for a period to continue with her studies.

When discussing this with her counsellor, she inadvertently used the words 'decree' and 'degree' interchangeably, often saying 'degree' when she meant 'decree' and vice versa. It was as though she came to university to get a degree but was going to leave with a decree instead. It was at this time likely that she would leave with the latter and not the former, which raised the interesting question of whether this was the underlying motivation for her return to study after all. Was she studying for the wrong reasons? Becoming a solicitor would enable her to divorce herself from an unsatisfactory life. In relation to her work she would find herself often having 'woolly thoughts' and asking herself, 'Why am I doing this?

It just doesn't make sense', which on reflection were exactly the same questions she was posing to herself in relation to her divorce. 'Am I being naive? Have I missed something?' were recurrent refrains in relation to constructing essays and her unease at being single again.

She had dealt with these anxieties during the separation by hurrying the divorce along, as a way of insuring against her fear of changing her mind. With it came an increasingly uncomfortable awareness that she might be a destructive person. In her search for something better, which she felt was purely selfish, she had 'destroyed her marriage' and put her children at risk, which functioned to put her in touch not only with her own hubris at wanting something better – and its possible disastrous consequences – but also with her mother, who, in attempting to better herself, had made herself less available to her family. No wonder Jean unconsciously equated academic work and the construction of an essay, particularly at the time of the final notification of the divorce, as a deconstruction of her family, making her both unavailable to her children and aware of an uncomfortable identification with a mother who became distracted by her academic aspirations. Jean too felt that at some level she might enjoy writing an essay more than being with the children, which was a truly frightening thought, with its implication that her mother might have felt the same. Academic work was either the most important thing in her life or the least important: Jean could not decide which.

The mature student rarely lacks motivation, but the psychological project, or consequence, may only become clear over time. Mature students cannot avoid being reminded – and having to rework – previous experiences of education, which not infrequently remind them of previous failures. A student who is mature is wanting to look forward in the service of a personal transformation, but in the process cannot help looking back.

Final transformations

A further opportunity for a particular form of transformation, whether conscious or unconscious, is death, especially if it is instigated and enacted by oneself. The student who attempts or commits suicide exerts a peculiarly morbid fascination which can be traced back through history. Suicide can involve the ultimate transformational fantasy: that we can rid ourselves of the familiar and become something else. Students and suicide have come to represent something heavily symbolic in our collective psyches. Young people who kill themselves, particularly if they are students, face us with the perennial and discomforting question of 'Why did he do it when he had everything to live for?' However, if we have everything to live for we have, by definition, everything to die for.

Students in higher education, that most privileged group, may be particularly vulnerable to suicidal gestures and acts. We have seen that students may need to subvert their successful or unsuccessful selves. Some form of self-harm may address that need. Apart from the developmental pressures during adolescence, the process of learning and knowledge itself may lead us to question and destroy what we feel we are becoming. While there is an increased vulnerability to suicide in adolescence and young adulthood, a seemingly disproportionate amount of attention is paid to students who kill themselves, a fact recognized by the Vienna Psychoanalytic Society (VPS) in 1910 during its deliberations on whether education is a contributory factor. Wilhelm Stekel, in a contribution to the discussions made at the time the radical suggestion that, 'I am inclined to feel that the principle of talion plays the decisive role here. No one kills himself who has never wanted to kill another, or at least wished the death of another . . .', and went on to suggest that the relationship between student and parent, or more importantly, the internalized parental figures, played a central part in suicide and suicidal gestures:

> The child wants to rob his parents of their greatest and most precious possession – his own life. The child knows that thereby he will inflict the greatest pain. Thus the punishment the child imposes on himself (his death) is simultaneously the punishment he imposes on the instigators of his sufferings (VPS 1910).

Stekel implies that suicide is linked with anger, and needs to be viewed in a relational context. This raises the question of who, or what, it is that our students are attempting to kill. Suicide can be a communication involving unsettled scores from childhood, as well as expressing ambivalence about the present. Despite our reluctance to acknowledge it, suicide involves dyads. Our difficulty in viewing suicide as a communication often involving hostile or negative thoughts may be an attempt to deny that these troublesome feelings exist or existed. The nature of the suicidal act is then denied, and the students who kill themselves are turned into innocent 'murder' victims. The hunt for the 'murderer' is then instigated, with education immediately becoming a suspect. That education is a prime suspect in this investigation is alluded to in a contribution by Freud to the VPS discussions, in which he suggests that '. . . schools ought to do something more than drive their pupils to suicide.' He was, in part, alluding to the widespread concern at that time with whether the Austrian educational system was excessively severe and damaging, but may well have been more prescient than even he imagined in raising both the connection between learning and suicide, as well as the nature and function of education. As a consequence the psychological meaning of the act is obscured, and an active act of self-harm is turned into something passively, and extraneously to the student, determined.

Young people who are both adolescent and studying are vulnerable to self-destructive thoughts. The question to live or to die is central to our lives, but it is perhaps especially in adolescence that the issue becomes so pressing. Many of the symptomatic presentations of students carry some risks, however disguised, to their lives. Eating problems, drug and alcohol abuse, self-harm and recklessness would come into this category. Although these forms of self-abuse do not contain the conscious wish to die (and thus do not necessarily have the same significance for the student) they may unconsciously represent similar preoccupations and thought processes to the explicitly suicidal. Similarly, not wanting to get up in the morning for a lecture, and the feelings associated with the sense of 'cannot be bothered', potentially reflect both feelings that the self does not want to continue and that the environment is not sufficiently enticing to evoke interest or attachment, thus inviting a hostile response. In a sense these are very real challenges both to the adult world and to education. If education is a preparation for life, then every student suicide is a challenge to that which is taught, and the possible lives on offer.

While for some suicide or thoughts of self-harm may be an adaptive response to unbearable pain and thus lead to a genuine desire to die, for others suicide and suicide attempts involve a transient loss of reality as a result of an intra-psychic split which makes the thought of self-destruction possible. A dyadic relationship is set up in fantasy between a part of the self which will survive (and thus is a denial of our physical destiny) and another part (often in adolescence associated with the body) which needs to be killed off. There always exists a belief that something will live on, which denies the reality of death.

At some level death is what happens to someone else; we all believe, despite evidence to the contrary, in our own immortality. The small child who, despite being angry with their parents and thinking, 'If I die you will be angry and upset, and then you will really love me', still believes they will survive.

In adolescence there exists a fantasy that we might have killed our bodies – or what they represent – but some other part of us will live on. We may thus be able via our own deaths to continue with our lives and studies, having successfully rid ourselves of that which has been experienced as difficult or problematic. This would link with the split view of our own mortality in suicidal acts and gestures. The suicidal student may well wish to die, but believe that it is only part of them that is going to die, a part often associated with the physical self. Another part will continue to live, ostensibly unaffected by the part which is killed off. Consequently a relationship is set up between a part of themselves that will survive and a part that will die. This, clearly, would have very practical implications for those tutoring, teaching, or treating, suicidal students. The psychological ability to do this requires a suspension of reality testing, and allows for two contradictory beliefs to co-exist. One way this may be facilitated is the romanticization of death in adolescence. Metaphors for death – as sleeping, or a tranquil rest – serve to deny the reality of death as a total cessation which is both final and irreversible. Culturally derived meanings of death which serve to deny or cushion our mortality, and notions of death as 'heroic' or 'peaceful' serve to make the inevitability of one's own death less frightening, but also aid thoughts that it might be something prematurely to aspire to. For adolescent students there may be certain attractions in controlling or making a statement about that which appears uncontrollably daunting.

Transition, change, separation, loss are variables which lower the threshold for suicide. Adolescent or young adult students are therefore particularly vulnerable. The process of transition itself may involve a certain form of suicide. It may be inevitable that any form of transition involves killing off something in ourselves in order to develop. Learning and developmental loss may evoke emotions associated with a young person having to take steps to actively renounce a cherished part of themselves. For some students that might, as we have seen, be more problematic than others. If development is ambivalently anticipated, then the part of us which feels ill-equipped or anxious about the progression to adulthood may wish to prematurely forestall or even terminate development altogether. Ambivalence about dependence and loss contribute to understanding why a suicide attempt is often preceded by an event which represents a failure in the move away from dependence on the parents, and the capacity to function independently. It is perhaps not surprising that students, preoccupied as they are with success or failure in so many areas of their lives – which represent acceptability or rejection and involve issues around the area of autonomy – ruminate so frequently about suicide. The success or failure in leaving home, the failure or sense of rejection of their first relationship, the success or failure in making friends, and the success or failure in examinations all contribute to the student's vulnerability. Associated as this is with the loss of the childhood self, the loss of the fantasy of a certain childlike innocence, and the ambivalence in respect of one's emerging sexual body, we can be lulled into believing that if we cannot control, or succeed in, other areas of our lives, at least we can control our physical selves. If bodies represent potentially uncomfortable feelings about sexuality or aggression which invoke excessive guilt, the young person may feel they deserve to be punished. Fantasies of dying are ways of addressing these issues. It is always possible that by destroying our bodies we are simultaneously persecuting the mind of another.

Separation from childhood or parents will provide the student with an unenviable choice. The dilemma is whether to attempt to stay merged with one's childhood, often represented by the parents, (which might be experienced as a form of psychic death in that you have to give up your own autonomy and independent self) or, at the other end of the spectrum, risk losing one's source of nurture and sustenance and become prematurely independent and self-sufficient. One way of resolving this is to contemplate suicide in the belief that the part of oneself that is plagued by this ambivalence will be killed off, leaving another part liberated from this dilemma and able to flourish.

Conversely, the fear of having lost a part of ourselves which is of value, the childhood self, say, may well lead us to view suicide as a way of reuniting ourselves with that which we fear we have lost, so that a suicide attempt may reflect a wish to remain or return to a state of unambivalent dependency. We might have to contemplate killing ourselves for our childhood to survive.

Loss and transition which is too rapid may provide the clues as to why someone should wish to contemplate killing themselves when they have 'everything to live for'. During the Vienna discussions, Freud listed some of the reasons why someone would wish to take their own life. These included guilt over hostile and aggressive wishes to others; psychic refusal to accept a loss; as an act of revenge; an escape from a real or perceived humiliation; a means of communication; and the person's identification with a suicidal parent. However, it was only with publication of 'Mourning and Melancholia' (1917) that the possible psychological mechanism was described. Freud suggested that loss is central to depressive states of mind, and he posited that when we lose someone or something of value we incorporate or introject that someone or something into ourselves. This may be an actual or imagined loss. We then have a memory of them that lives on in our minds, which may even become part of ourselves, as frequently happens when our parents die.

Suicide becomes a possibility via the mechanism of excessive or punishing guilt. Since ambivalence to that which is lost or has deserted us is central to the process of mourning, we will have to deal with our hostility, and consequent guilt, to the lost person or object. Frequently the negative side of this ambivalence is consciously denied, leaving it to torment us unconsciously. Anger then becomes directed at that part of our mind that represents or symbolizes the lost person or object. This anger, a product of our ambivalence, exists in our minds and, since it evokes guilt, is consciously defended against. Hostility against the lost person or object, which becomes magnified and aroused by the loss, is now reversed and pointed back against the self. Self-reproach – so common in depressed and suicidal states of mind – can then be seen as reproaches against the loved or lost object which, via guilt, have been reversed and pointed against the self. We may try and kill ourselves rather than someone else. 'Daddy', the striking poem by Sylvia Plath – who did eventually take her own life – graphically illustrates some of these factors. In the poem she alludes to both her affection and anger towards her deceased father, describing her marriage as an attempt to find a father substitute, where the ambivalence can continue to be enacted. Her own suicide could be seen in this light as a reunion with Daddy – that is, the reverse side of this ambivalence; that our death will reunite us with someone we loved. If we feel we did not love them enough there exists the possibility that we may seek our own deaths as a way of making reparation to them or dealing with our guilt.

Alternatively, suicide may be an attempt at a certain form of altruism. It can act to protect the ambivalently loved person from what rightly or wrongly the suicidal individual fears he is about to do. In this sense suicide would be a defence against murder. Thoughts of killing ourselves as a result of falling behind in our academic work, or the number of essays we owe or are outstanding, may be ways we protect those who have made those demands of us from the consequences of our rage.

We all consciously or unconsciously have a special relationship with death. The paradox at adolescence is that during a period in our lives when we are in general in good health, the possibility of dying becomes almost seductive and viewed as a cure for life. At that time we may conceive of death in a rather romanticized way, often with alluring visions of merging with nature. It is a period in our lives when being reunited with Mother Earth has some attractions. The hope or possibility of being reunited with something or someone may also speak to the excruciating loneliness of adolescence (and studying) and help us deal with the anxieties consequent upon the realization of being on our own.

Our own relationship to death may be secretly nurtured and exist in an at times split-off and disassociated fantasy of what our deaths will facilitate. These subjective fantasies may take various forms. The following description of suicidal fantasies is a brief account of some of these fantasies (Campbell and Hale, 1991). The 'merging fantasy' would include a return to nature, becoming one with the universe, and a return to mother in an inorganic state. If your body is the major obstacle to that it may fuel the belief that by killing off the body your mind will survive, lessening the possibility of seeing suicide as a total annihilation of the self. The 'revenge fantasy', getting your own back or getting your retaliation in first, would focus on the impact your death will have on others. To be successful this fantasy needs to incorporate the continued existence of the self, if only to be able to obtain maximum satisfaction from witnessing the distress of others at one's own death. Revenge and triumph ensure that sadism is never far from the surface in this fantasy. Fantasies of self-punishment can deal with excessive sexualized guilt by killing off the source of the guilty suffering: the body. The 'elimination fantasy' will rid you of something that is problematic, even driving you mad, while you survive, whereas a 'dicing-with-death' fantasy would entail placing yourself at some physical risk, partly to provoke a certain response from others, but also to attack the other by putting your body or mind (particularly if part of it symbolically represents someone else) at risk.

Simplistically one could say that while the potentially violent person feels intruded upon by others and lashes out, the potentially suicidal or self-harming person, betrayed by a certain form of abandonment, is compelled to act against the self. Student suicidal fantasies are generally multi-causal, but as a result of ambivalence and the fantasy that a certain part of the young person will survive, often involve some transformational desire or intent:

> The student who felt bemused as to why he felt like killing himself was the student who discovered at an advanced age, through conversations with an elder sister, that he had had an elder brother who died in a boating accident at the age of two. He was born shortly afterwards, and the incident was never talked about, despite his mother's self-evident grief and preoccupation. He had always been dimly aware of a certain unease in himself which seemed paradoxically to be intensified, rather than relieved, by his academic success, in which neither he nor his mother could take much satisfaction. His mother had always been preoccupied with his health, but seemingly unaware of his 'real existence'. He was not sure he was allowed or could allow himself to live, other than merely be, and had become, in fantasy at least, preoccupied upon his sister's communication with issues including: whether he was a 'replacement child' and able to have any independent identity; guilt

that he had usurped his brother's place and proved to be an unsatisfactory replacement; and whether he was destined to have the same fate as his brother. A mother's unsuccessful transformational wish had been unconsciously communicated to her son, who could only comply by contemplating suicide; a transformation that would magically ensure that his brother's memory could live on in his mother's mind unsullied by disappointing comparisons with himself. The tragedy of the 'replacement child' is that their function may be merely to exist rather than to live. For this student, his mere existence was in itself a reproach to others.

Suicide as a form of identification with that which is lost can be seen in its theoretical rudimentary form in 'The Psychopathology of Everyday Life' (1901), where Freud comments on the death of a military officer in a riding 'accident' a few months after the death of his mother. The mechanisms of grief, guilt and identification are outlined as precursors of suicidal behaviours and 'fatal accidents'. Suicidal or self-harming transformations in education can function in a variety of ways, aided by psychological splitting. By killing off the part of us that is ignorant we can believe that our cleverness will live on in a transformed state. Conversely, if we find our increasing knowledge disturbing we may seek to ensure that it is destroyed in the service of a negative transformational project. Transformations need not always be positive.

Education offers a template for positive or self-destructive transformations to occur. It is overseas students, who are literally in transition from one culture to another, for whom transformations are most acute and challenging. How does this process manifest itself for students who have left their homelands and mother tongues? To begin to understand this we may need to look at the split between minds and bodies. It is to this matter that we now turn.

5
Foreign bodies

. . . her pure and eloquent blood
spoke in her cheekes, and so distincktly wrought,
that one might almost say her bodie thought.

John Donne, 'Progress of the Soul', 1633

How can we avoid thinking? Or, to put it another way, do we always have to think with our minds? What are the methods available to us for communicating affective states? If our first experience of ourselves is essentially a somatic one, that is, our developmentally earliest ego is a body ego, then could we under certain conditions revert to using our bodies to think or to speak for us?

Our thirst for knowledge is initially directed towards knowing about our own, or others', bodies. A certain curiosity about the body and its uses, both in terms of its function and its potential for communication, becomes linked in some form with the more sophisticated ability to be curious about intellectual concepts and the world around us. If we view curiosity about the body as a developmentally rudimentary stage, to be eventually transformed into a more sophisticated mental curiosity, we may be close to understanding the split between psyche and soma. If we are able, or are inevitably led, to split psyche and soma, then other splits, not least that between intellect and emotions, become possible. Curiosity of the mind replaces curiosity of the body; but we never lose a fascination, if not preoccupation, with our physical selves. Under pressure, thinking with our bodies may be the way we avoid thinking with our minds.

Somatic expression

Throughout our lives we may deal with emotional tension via ways that depend less on language and are characteristic of earlier forms of functioning. Modes of thinking and experiencing in infancy are essentially speechless, although laden with powerful emotional significance. It is interesting to note the prevalence of bodily metaphors when describing emotional states, e.g. tremble in fear, crushed in sorrow, choked with anger (McDougall, 1989). Psychosomatic ailments may represent a primitive kind of body language, where the task becomes interpreting a language which does not use words. If we need to circumvent the use of words in order to communicate, it may present a particularly intruiging dilemma in education where words are often the sole arbiters of discourse. Education may well encourage a certain dissociation between words and emotions. Thinking with our emotions appears an educational tautology, if not a pedagogic crime. The tutor is faced with a physical obstacle to learning in the student, be it a headache or double vision, while the student's exclusive preoccupation is with an ailment which urgently seeks and resists translation. Students who have no words to describe these emotional states of mind need to be able to find pathways for a somatic experience to become intelligible in the service of learning. The difficulty is most problematic when there is no discharge for our affective lives other than through our bodies. If language of the body is a substitute for some form of symbolic mental representation involving thought or emotional pain, it follows that in education we need to listen to a language which might be foreign although not alien:

> Ian, an enigmatic and intense 18 year old, reluctantly agreed to be referred for counselling after months of unsuccessful physical investigations of his various physical symptoms, which included concern about a possible brain tumour, muscle fatigue, lethargy and non-specific weakness involving tiredness and low spirits. This led Ian to withdraw both from his friends and from his studies at university for a period, and retreat to a rather debilitating existence at home where his presence was reciprocally unwelcome to both himself and his parents.
>
> He came from an aspiring family in which his brusque father expected much of him, becoming volubly disenchanted with him when he failed to live up to expectations. Ian's attentive and adoring mother 'fussed' over him, particularly in relation to his physical safety and appearance, and tended to think for him. 'As a scientist' (he was studying biochemistry), he saw himself as a logical, ordered young man, who had diagnosed himself as suffering from an organic syndrome which he knew existed, but which successive doctors had misdiagnosed. It was a consequence of the failure of these physicians that he was 'sent for' counselling. He had always been a precociously clever child, whose esteem among his peers depended heavily upon his wit and guile, which had functioned to mask his low self-confidence. Faddy and ostensibly self-sufficient as an adolescent, he had begun to be concerned in the sixth form about recurrent headaches and 'thought it was the beginning of brain rot', which, since it resulted in poorer academic and social performance, led to decreasing social

approval. His brain was his 'vital' (and over-valued) organ, and needed to be protected at all cost, which led him to, among other things, avoid travelling in cars since his 'brain would shake'. Subjective misery was denied, but he admitted to being angry and frustrated as a result of the failure of the medical profession to successfully diagnose and treat his illness. He knew what medication he needed, if only others would prescribe it for him. Belligerence was his predominant emotion, but when I suggested that he may be depressed, he readily agreed, saying what was depressing was the reluctance of his G.P. to prescribe for him!

The fact that Ian was able to comprehend if not accept the concept of depression – or the notion of the psychological – led him eventually to the realization that what he was suffering from was growing up, and what was instrumental in this self-discovery was passing his driving test. He could now drive himself wherever he wanted without his brain being shaken up by being driven by another. The unthinkable had become thinkable.

What happens, then, for students who come from a culture or subculture where the concept of the psychological either does not exist, or the symbolic meaning of dis- or un-ease is perceived in a totally different framework? Students from cultures, foreign or indigenous, where there is no concept of the psychological, will inevitably have different ways of communicating anxiety.

Mohammed, a post-graduate student from the Middle East, had developed tension headaches and a variety of psychosomatic symptoms shortly after his arrival in Britain. Bemused and unsure what counselling was and what form of examination I was to subject him to, this tall, broad, and ungainly 30-year-old man, appeared both preoccupied and miserable. Arriving explaining that he had recently had an EEG which proved negative, he now thought a brain scan was indicated as his symptoms implied, as he had been informed by Western friends, a tumour. Clearly perplexed why his doctor had suggested he come and see me, he relaxed slightly at my suggestion that it is sometimes helpful to get a variety of opinions. He explained that he had recently arrived in this country – his arrival matching the onset of his headaches – from the capital of his home country where he worked as an academic at the university. It was impossible for him to progress in his career without completing his graduate studies overseas. He was a married man whose family, including a baby born since his arrival in Britain, had been left at home for the duration of his studies. There were no signs of a clinical depression and all other areas of his life were going fine. 'If it wasn't for the headaches I would really enjoy my studies and living in your country.' He further revealed that when he sat down to study, he would be struck by double vision and unable to read. I suggested that he had a lot to contend with: leaving his family and friends, transition to this country, including housing difficulties, language, and cultural differences, and being trapped by his studies. He had to succeed before he could go back to his country, yet could not read. At this he looked at me with a mixture of blank incomprehension and incredulity. These were not problems, he replied somewhat petulantly, and were easily surmountable if only his headaches would stop. I suggested that there was possibly a physical and psychological aspect to his headaches. He needed to reassure himself that there was no physical cause for his complaints while at the same time looking at how incapacitating the headaches were and what effect they were having on his spirits. Could it be that they were in part the effects of cumulative stress, and that they were his body's way of communicating anxiety as a warning which needed practical attention? He replied that some months ago his optician had prescribed a pair of glasses that he suspected were too strong for him (a response not without interest to the proceeding formulation) and that he would return to his optician and contact me again if necessary.

I never saw Mohammed again. Tutors and counsellors can be colonized by their assumptions the moment an overseas student walks into the room.

Geoffrey, a 22-year-old student from central Africa, had failed his exams and wished to repeat the year. His tutor was unsure, given his health, whether that was advisable. Geoffrey, a rather cowed, seemingly besieged young man, explained that he had regular panic attacks, breathing difficulties where he would be unable to breathe for some 30 seconds, and heart palpitations which convinced him that he was suffering from an undiagnosed cardiac complaint. He was losing weight, and was only eating one meal a day as he could not afford more. He was embittered and disappointed at the hand life had dealt him, and now no one was taking his life-threatening illness seriously. He had been to see his G.P., who had told him he was suffering from anxiety and worry. He could not understand the former concept, while he did not feel worried about anything apart from his cardiac complaint and being able to repeat the year.

'If I could receive proper treatment for my heart, I would be able to study and pass my examinations.'

He had come from an affluent family, and when 16 had been sent to Britain to attend a public school to complete his A-levels. After some 18 months, his family were unable to send further money out of the country, and Geoffrey had to leave the school and attend a local comprehensive. He failed his A-levels, returned to his country, married, and returned to Britain to complete an Access course, working nightly in petrol station forecourts. He had to get, i.e. passively receive, a Western education. As with Mohammed, Geoffrey had, through Western eyes, suffered many disruptions and losses in the process of studying abroad, yet had no psychological or sociological context in which to frame his experience. It could be said that this lack of framework was shared by his tutors, G.P., and counsellor, who were equally unable to make sense of or understand his dilemma. Trapped as he appeared to be, unable to return to his own country without a degree, yet unable to actively master his studies, it was as though his physical complaint provided both a refuge and an extremely unsatisfactory, and very temporary, compromise.

Symptoms, perhaps particularly psychosomatic ailments, may generally be viewed as attempts at a self-cure. Something is wrong that needs to be put right. They have the function of binding anxiety extremely successfully. For overseas students, they may also serve to deflect reservations or criticisms from an imperfect external world on to imperfect or deficient bodies. Both Mohammed and Geoffrey denied any difficulty or reservations about other areas of their lives socially, culturally, academically, racially or linguistically if only the pain would stop. What was also curious was the apparent lack of affect in these encounters, which suggested not only psychoanalytic heresy, but also that a certain absence was something that the students were themselves feeling in relation to a foreign culture. The demand to be counselled was in many ways similar to the demand made on them by their education. Needing to acquire an English education, in part to effect a personal transformation, was in some measure distracting these students from their own development. Getting an English education was synonymous with getting counselling for their symptom; both were impossible demands dealt with by silence or bewilderment. The demand itself was bewildering. The therapeutic and educational task was imperious in nature. A model and ideology was being surreptitiously imposed on a reluctant student. This matched the way the body via physical symptoms colonized the mind.

Finding a cultural idiom

In these instances the need is to understand the subjective affective language of the student and how emotional states are expressed in his or her culture. This raises the question of whether the notion of affect is itself translatable. The fact that language, including an emotional vocabulary, evolves in part according to certain environmental conditions, suggests that with these students, particularly those from different cultures, the task is to discover the personal or cultural idiom:

Ayoda was a petite, well-dressed, fashionable woman in her late 20s. She explained her symptoms in a distant, detached manner, before lapsing into silence. She had suffered for some time from double vision, heart palpitations, hyperventilation, which had led to an erratic sleep pattern and interfered with her work, leading her to withdraw from people. She was worried lest her health gave way, and was convinced she suffered from a chronic heart or neurological condition which would prevent her from completing her higher degree. Previous investigations had not reassured her. Double vision as a symptom can itself be of interest, as it implies that one identical view is superimposed on another which may assume symbolic significance for overseas students. Born in West Africa, into a large ostensibly Christian family, her father had four wives, of whom Ayoda's mother was the first. Ayoda was the third of five children. Her younger sisters were also studying in Britain. From the ages of one to eleven, Ayoda had been cared for by various relatives, often in distant parts of the country. At age 11 she was sent to a boarding school where she 'supposed' she was happy (happiness being a concept she was having some difficulty with). At age 16 she was sent to a girls' public school in Britain to study for her A-levels, which she completed successfully before return-ing home to complete her undergraduate degree.

Her father had been an extremely successful businessman owning an airline, who had died suddenly from a heart attack when Ayoda was 16 and at public school. She returned home briefly for the funeral but had resumed her studies soon after. A few months later she had 'inexplicably' become upset at boarding school but had quickly been cheered up by her matron.

Her father had given things to children who succeeded and beat those who did not. She had always been his favourite and successful daughter, which was now in jeopardy as a result of her inability to study. Interestingly, Ayoda's research interest was associated with aviation law and the penalties that a charterer would pay for failing to fulfil a contract. This mirrored her desperation to complete her doctorate. From one, but not the only, perspective her symptom could represent an attempted identification with her deceased father, but also a way of keeping him alive. Her father had died intestate, leaving confusion and acrimony among the relatives. Her mother, who had when younger aspirations to become a lawyer, abandoned these on her marriage, and was seen by Ayoda as very strong, coping with anything that life could throw at her. Consequently, Ayoda viewed her own symptoms as both an accusation and a communication from her mother; she had to cope and was perplexed why she was becoming so agitated. It may well be, again viewed from a specific standpoint, that this suggested an unconscious wish to fail as a protest against Ayoda's colonization by both mother and the demand of acquiring an English education.

Ayoda was confused in many areas of her life, not least in her belief system and the issue of her identity. Her family had belonged to a number of clans whose unifying force had always been religion, specifically the worship of a number of pagan gods, who were worshipped even among her wider family, who were considered to be among the Christian elite. Belief in reincarnation, destiny, and illness associated with bad spirits of one's forebears were particularly strong. Her grandparents' view of death was that 'the dead are not alive but still exist' as a spiritual presence watching over and admonishing descendants. Frequently a god would single out a person by fighting with them, causing physical or mental illness or some other misfortune. Belief in reincarnation was central, the identity of the reincarnated ancestor being physical resemblance or similarity. Ayoda related this in a manner which suggested this was a historical fiction, and that none of this applied to her. However it became apparent that values which I, subconsciously at least, held to be self-evident (autonomy, self-development, privacy, or even the right to happiness) were not shared by Ayoda's extended family, who, despite her latent protestations, were still exerting considerable power over her. The world of affects, internal worlds, and emotional experiences were linked to spirits, gods, and presences. These existed outside oneself, not owned and certainly not reflected on; what indeed was there to reflect on?

Ayoda came from a culture where men were assumed to be naturally polygamous, so it was preferable to institutionalize this to protect the women. Traditionally wives could not inherit from their husbands, the inheritance passing on to the children, often on the basis of the eldest, but frequently on the basis of those felt to be most worthy. Despite the appearance of a Western-educated Christian family, Ayoda came from a tradition in which the primacy of the lineage placed emphasis on group socialization with and by peers in child rearing rather than with biological parents. As a result of children being highly valued, their care was seen as a general rather than a personal concern. Development was viewed as axiomatic, and the child thought to grow up in a relatively untroubled way. Children were not thought of in individual developmental terms, but viewed as adapting easily to new situations and readily putting unpleasant experiences behind them. Children were often named according to either the circumstances of their birth, or certain familial expectations. Ayoda was called 'Special One', which was particularly resonant, given the expectations of her.

Clearly this put Ayoda's blurred vision and difficulty breathing into a somewhat different context. Issues around the role of women and marriage, multiple caretakers in childhood, child care, death and reincarnation, spiritual beliefs, the function and purpose of education had (despite her protestations that, as someone who was being educated in the West, she no longer believed in 'all this') a culturally ambiguous meaning for Ayoda. Much of Ayoda's symptomatology became slightly more understandable in the context of the culture from which she came, and her desperate struggle to integrate these seemingly impossible belief systems.

Psychological theories that take their starting point solely in the behaviour and psychopathology of individuals may well have little to offer students from, in this case, West Africa. Ayoda's problem, and perhaps the plight of all those being educated abroad, is the dislocation and dissociation inherent in any educational migration. In Ayoda's case, this took the form of a pressing need to negate her past and culture while simultaneously being haunted by it, in the sense that it provided a more authentic explanation of her predicament than any Western psychological theory. Caught between the idiom of the world she had temporarily left behind, and the Western philosophical and literary tradition of her host nation – with its emphasis on a certain kind of introspection, including a capacity to reflect – Ayoda and overseas students in general may be more susceptible to talking with their bodies.

This need to know something of the personal idiom applies equally to indigenous students, particularly those from minority backgrounds, but with students from different cultures who have migrated for education, the cultural differences may not include the idea of a personal idiom, private self, or any concept such as an individual psychology which can symbolically express or translate ill-health into un- or dis-ease.

Body language

Mohammad, Geoffrey, and Ayoda were overseas students, very Western in their appearance, manners and thinking, who had succeeded in their own Western-orientated educational systems. Despite this they needed to integrate, not jettison or deny, their cultural heritage. Studying abroad acted for them as a return of the repressed. What these students repressed is part of themselves; in Ayoda's case this was her Africanness, her belief in tradition, her lineage, her archaic self. The repressed returned as a pain, a longing, a disconnectedness which became freed from anxiety by a physical symptom which enabled her to withdraw from the external world, including Britain and university, into a personal difficulty of mastering an environment whose demands were at some level alien to her.

Bodies are in some ways an effective language for conveying overseas students' dis-ease. It may also be that part of the terror of losing the symptom, so prevalent in psychosomatic ailments, is bound up with a fear that overseas students may get in touch with a terrific longing for a culture they have left, and become very critical of a culture they have arrived in. In this the symptom provides a focus: what would these students be thinking about if they did not have a symptom?

Developments in education may accentuate a tendency to use our bodies in this way. For overseas students in particular, the transition in the host nation's perception of them (from being a benevolent responsibility – particularly those coming from countries associated with Britain's Imperial past – to a more functional, if not ruthless, view of them as consumers of a product termed an 'overseas education') may well encourage the somatization of anxiety. Given the somewhat indecent rush to recruit overseas students, and the versions of the host nation they are increasingly being sold, what kind of symptomatology has to be adopted by a student under stress coming from a culture where the affective language (anxiety, depression, even mental illness) is very different from our own? Could it be that body language is the only way some students can talk to us?

The project of migration for education is in itself a curious one which has existed throughout history:

> You are aware that a multitude of scholars from diverse parts meets at our town for study, which we hold a very gratifying and desirable thing . . . since no small benefit and glory accrues

therefrom to our whole realm. Unless you conduct yourself with more restraint and moderation towards them they will be driven by your exactations to leave your town, abandoning their studies, and leave the country which we by no means desire . . . (Henry III addressing the people of Cambridge, 1231).

. . .[the] rain never stopped, the heating failed, the landlady was racist, the student counselling service unsympathetic, the medical centre did not take my ailments seriously, I met no one, my research was handicapped by linguistic misunderstandings, and the return flight was overbooked. (An overseas student's account of his experience.)

Despite the centuries separating these two quotations it is tempting to believe that very little has changed. On the one hand the uneasy balance between altruism and self-interest on the donor's part, and on the other the desperate anguish of the, presumed grateful, recipient. The demand on the student to manage migration for education is superimposed on the need to adapt (but not too well, as your migration is only temporary, and this distinguishes this form of migration from others) and to learn. When familiar cues are removed, and unfamiliar ones substituted, students may feel at best a minor sense of discomfort until they have come to terms with the new demands made on them, while at worst experience a sense of acute disorientation which they feel ill-equipped to manage. Strategies which worked for the overseas student in the home culture may be attempted but found wanting in the host culture. Fantasies of homogeneity, including the denial of difference, in both student and host may prove problematic. Migration is stressful, and safe value judgements about cultural dissonance often associated with overseas students are often erroneous and unhelpful.

Overseas students, like indigenous ones, are not static, and are living through a process which can be broken down to its component parts. Becoming an overseas student begins prior to departure, with its characteristic mixture of elation and anticipatory anxiety, while being an overseas student inevitably, despite a possibly brief honeymoon period, involves a sense of loss of what has had to be given up and what has been left behind. Symptoms can often emerge during this period when adaptation is either attempted or avoided. Numbness, anger, guilt at leaving one's country behind, idealization (or denigration) of either the home country or the host country can lead to a form of mourning similar to a bereavement. Concern about the possible costs of what a successful adaptation may entail may also be in evidence at this stage. Will it involve a transformation which will make the inevitable return problematic? Educational migration in this sense involves a particular kind of trauma. Maintaining a sense of continuous identity can be especially problematic.

Excessive guilt in relation to those that have been left behind may take the form of attempts to make reparation via an intense preoccupation with the safety of those at home. Alternatively, refuge from punitive guilt is sought through self-punishment in an illness, real or imagined. Overseas students may have to learn, or become more competent in, a new language, distancing them from the mother tongue and reinforcing a sense of separation, if not alienation. The return home, particularly if successful, may evoke pleasure but may bring with it a recognition that the student has changed in a way that makes the task of reintegration more problematic. Institutional and societal factors can aid or impede this process.

For students presenting with physical ailments of no known aetiology, the symptom becomes an imperialist: a despotic emperor who holds absolute sway and exerts supreme control over the psyche. In this the symptom is a form of self-domination. If education demands some degree of compliance from students, it may well be that these students can make their minds but not their bodies comply. The body via the symptom is then exploited to tell the truth. Being 'ill' may be a way of making sense of our lives. Education needs to take some cognizance of an intermediate world, between past-present, psyche-soma, intellect-emotions (which frequently mirrors – if not is instigated by – the mind-body split) and recognize the conflicting psychic and social demands which need to be negotiated for learning to take place:

Michael, a courteous, affable man in his mid-20s, explained that he did not think I could help, but was desperate for some way out of his predicament. He suffered from diffuse spinal pain, headaches, breathing difficulties and double vision, as a result of which he was unable to sit down and concentrate on his studies. He had undergone extensive investigations at a variety of teaching hospitals which had revealed no physical cause.

He came from a large semi-affluent family in East Africa and had had a variety of caretakers as a child. He explained he had always been successful in his studies, a diligent and hard-working student, and had won a prestigious scholarship to study abroad. He was very excited by this, particularly as a successful completion of his course would qualify him for an eminent position on his return home, but was hamstrung by his physical complaints. He could not conceive of having a pain of no organic origin. Although his symptoms had begun soon after his arrival in Britain, no causal connection was made. Again the function of the symptom was to bind other possible anxieties. Everything else – poor housing, loneliness, homesickness, the cool response of English people – was of little consequence. If only the symptom would be diagnosed and treated, these could be mastered. His health was a total and exclusive preoccupation.

After some time he volunteered that prior to leaving home he thought he had contracted malaria and, unsure whether he had actually caught the disease, his mother had convinced him to consult a traditional witchdoctor. What was of interest was the way in which this was communicated to me: coyly and awkwardly, suggesting he did not believe in such things – of course they were nonsense but we need to keep our mothers happy – an uncomfortable compromise between his African roots and his Western education. Giggling slightly with embarrassment, he confided that the witchdoctor had suggested that demons had possessed him and needed to be exorcized, and that he take a number of potions, maintain a number of culinary prohibitions and eat only food prepared under the supervision of his mother. Surprisingly, he said he did feel better but was unable to continue with the treatment on his arrival in Britain. At my suggestion that it sounded as if he was ashamed that an educated and cultivated person like himself be helped by a witchdoctor, he readily agreed, saying yes, it did not make any sense (nor, at some level, did the need to study abroad). In the light of this I suggested that psychological explanations for his pain were perhaps the Western equivalent of witchcraft – both did not make any sense, but might be of help. Jointly agreeing to this proposition we went on to have nonsensical conversations.

If two of the possible dilemmas in this area are, what is a (British) education a cure for?, or what version of myself do I want to become via a (British) education?, then the overseas student is immediately confronted with the notion of education as an object of both transition and transformation.

Fundamental to the discussion so far is the importance of acknowledging difference. Students, whether graduate, mature, or from overseas, need to be comfortable with their differences and have them valued by education. However, it is in relation to gender where this may prove most problematic, and it is to this subject that we now turn.

6
Gender

I was as a girl suffering a degree of colonization of the mind. Especially (in) writing I'd (quite) unconsciously posit a male point of view as the general one. So there was an element of the male impersonator about this young person as she was finding herself (Angela Carter, *Death of the Author*, 1992).

In conformity with its peculiar nature, psychoanalysis does not try to describe what a woman is – that would be a task it could scarcely perform – but sets about inquiring how she comes into being (Sigmund Freud, 1933).

Freud neglected to ask how a woman comes into possession of her own story, becomes a subject, when even narrative convention assigns her the place of an object of desire. How does an object tell a story? (Bernheimer and Kahane, 1985).

Jenny was a lively effervescent young undergraduate biochemist who consulted a counsellor out of a sense of bewildered concern. Both her boyfriend and her doctor had suggested that she 'come for counselling' (as though counselling is something one has done to one) as she had this 'irritating little habit' of plucking out her eyebrows and pulling out clumps of her hair. This was related in a somewhat bemused and embarrassed fashion; it was not an issue of great importance, yet other people did notice and it 'niggled' away at her in a particularly infuriating fashion. She immediately went on to say that 'my mother is a hairdresser'. I found myself almost involuntarily raising my eyebrows to which she said, '. . . it all began when I was about 16, and my mother thinks it started when I became interested in boys.' It would appear that in these first few exchanges this young woman was revealing something important of herself.

    The story that Jenny went on to tell (and in which Jenny featured as an object in a narrative of her changing body) was quite simply that her mother was a hairdresser who believed that she was too interested in boys, and that Jenny pulled her hair out. Could there be a link? It was of interest that when Jenny's symptom occurred – often at home in the presence of her mother – her mother would immediately notice, and after scolding Jenny would burst into tears and run away into another part of the house.

Jenny was the first member of her family to go to university 'let alone study science'. Her father was a self-employed mechanic, described by Jenny as an affable, passive, and amusing man. While conveying her affection for him, Jenny gave the impression that he was, in terms of the parental couple, of minor consequence. Mother was much more dominant, unpredictable, strict, and given to explosive tempers. Jenny had a younger sister who 'was not very bright but seen by my parents as nice'. Jenny was immediately confronted with the interesting conundrum, was it possible for a daughter to be 'bright and nice'?

'In the family I am the genius but my sister has the pleasanter personality.' While saying this, Jenny was alive to what she had earlier said about her parents: father amusing and pleasant but ineffectual, mother highly strung, volatile, but formidably dominant. In one sense Jenny was talking about her own identification: who she was more like, and where the problem may be located.

She had attended an independent girls' sixth-form, which she enjoyed, but boys 'were a problem'. The problem being that boys were interested in her and she in them. She had a 'hectic nightlife', but her choice of boyfriends always infuriated her mother. A succession of unemployed men, all considerably older than Jenny, were brought home, and purposely introduced to Jenny's parents for their – especially mother's – disapproval. The effect on her mother was that she would 'shriek' her disapproval and disappear.

Was it possible for a woman to be clever and sexual? A seemingly bizarre and irrational symptom was beginning to be linked with a young woman's wish to defy her mother. Jenny's relationship with her mother was central to her preoccupations. Initially, when talking about her uneasy relationship with her mother, Jenny thought that this occurred because they were so unalike; Jenny suspected that her mother preferred her younger sister who, although not as clever, was thought considerably 'nicer'. Jenny had always felt that communication with her mother was a problem. She felt different and the odd one out in her family, and had during her younger adolescence flung herself into activities outside the home in order to feel less 'odd' and abnormal. This had the effect of incurring mother's disapproval. Jenny's 'oddness' was a way that she was communicating with her mother in the context of a relationship where the problem was similarity rather than difference. How could a hairdresser-mother compete with a daughter who was in the process of not having any hair? How could a clever daughter allow herself to compete or feel comfortable with a mother who left school at 16?

Although Jenny came to see how similar temperamentally she

was to her mother (and that this was the problem rather than the opposite), there were major areas of reproach: her mother had always appeared distant and preoccupied, and it was difficult for Jenny to explore areas of similarity and difference without mother becoming critical and accusatory. Boys and hair appeared to be the only forum for Jenny to communicate with the one person in the family with whom she desperately needed to communicate.

The 'issue' of her eyebrows also contained within it a form of symbolic representation of a wish to escape from an intrusive mother while still maintaining an identification with a mother who was experienced as impressively similar. Controlling her hair was both a channel for negotiation with her real and internalized mother, as well as an area, unlike academic work and relationships, where Jenny felt supremely in control and able to influence her own destiny. Unbeknown to Jenny she was engaged in re-enacting some of her mother's unconscious conflicts around definitions about what it is to be a woman with an independent identity in a culture whose idiom of an autonomous woman is fraught with ambivalence. It was at times unclear whether Jenny's hair – the subject of the story – was an object belonging to her or her mother.

Jenny was never clear whether by surpassing her mother in her academic attainments or her success with boys she was becoming different (and attacking her) or staying the same (enacting a maternally approved script).

Margaret's dilemma was not dissimilar:

> Margaret was a 33-year-old graduate student who, within a chapter of finishing her thesis, became depressed and unable to write coherently. After spending four years on her thesis this was clearly a major problem. Margaret was the elder of two children of a humble West Country family. Her father died when she was 13, and Margaret and her younger brother were brought up by her mother, who worked as a midwife and had not remarried. Margaret had done well at school, but had become depressed while an undergraduate. Deciding at that point not to pursue an academic career, she worked for a time in publishing, but had a further depressive episode in her late 20s just at the time when she had become engaged to be married. The marriage was called off, and Margaret decided to return to her studies, welcoming a more reflective life. It rapidly became apparent that Margaret still mourned the loss of her father, who she could barely remember, but in retrospect recalled him as being enigmatically exciting and different from the family's culture of reserved gentility.

She viewed herself as a rather plain, intense woman who would not evoke much interest from another; she would idly speculate that had she been more interesting, lively, or engaging her father would still be alive. Thirteen-year-old daughters, Margaret thought, needed to evoke and maintain an ardent interest from and in their fathers. Her relationship with her mother had remained tense and uneasy, revolving around issues of competition and rivalry in relation to academic success and maternal procreativity. On the latter her midwife mother proved unassailable, while on the former Margaret was never entirely comfortable with her undoubted superior attainments.

In her initial consultation Margaret had used the phrases 'time is running out' and feeling 'physically sick' in relation to her thesis, which on reflection led to our speculation that her thesis was the baby she never had, which made her reluctance to relinquish it perfectly understandable. Over the last four to five years she had so tenderly nurtured it; no wonder she did not want to let go of it. This was a phantom-thesis baby as opposed to the real baby she wished for: relinquishing this baby now would be like effectively killing it off. Margaret related to herself 'as if' she were her mother. Never 'leaving' her doctorate enabled her to remain in a benign and therefore non-rivalrous identification with a mother who, through her midwifery, never left the care and delivery of successive generations of children; her doctorate was the one child who would always remain at the point of delivery. To relinquish her doctorate would bring her into competition with a mother who had babies. The current paralysis enabled Margaret to continue to define herself as unlike her mother (academic) while at the same time as similar to her (a woman continually at the point of having – or delivering – babies). Margaret was never quite sure whether her current inertia was the result of an attack on her own abilities or whether it functioned as a resentful identification with her mother, which would deal with the uncomfortable feelings of loss Margaret would face if she 'succeeded' in being more successful – that is different from – her mother. Unease with mother over babies and careers – procreativity and creativity – and the pervasive issue of loss, which for Margaret included the risk in any potentially successful relationship, which might produce a real baby, of replacing her foreclosed and fantasized relationship with her father, led to a paralysis in her life just at a time when the comforts of economic security and the possibility of a moderately successful relationship were beckoning.

Margaret was involved in a relationship with a man who, as a result of geographic separation, she saw intermittently. She found this both vaguely unsatisfactory and acceptable. To be closer would not only risk her secretly nurtured relationship with her deceased father, but would also paradoxically threaten the relationship since she believed that her boyfriend (a computer programer and 'not at all academic') harboured a fear of the powerful academic woman which she represented. Margaret feared that closer proximity and intimacy would be experienced by him as invasive and provoke his possible flight, which, as a result of Margaret's experience – or lack of it – with her father, had to be avoided at all cost. Whether this was an accurate perception of the reality of her situation was unclear; what became clearer was that Margaret's perception of herself as an academic woman was intrinsically connected with an internalization of an invasive, powerful, and potentially destructive femininity from which others needed protection. Whether men disliked intellectual women (making Margaret's hesitation at the point of receiving confirmation that she was one understandable) was immaterial: Margaret distrusted them. Who needs an enemy when one has access to an internal saboteur?

The formation of gender identity, attitude, and expectation is a curious mix of emotional, biological, cognitive, and environmental factors, resulting as we have seen from the reciprocal interaction between the self, environment, and others.

Masculine, feminine

Freud believed that the perception of ourselves as masculine and feminine arose out of the unavoidable recognition of our anatomical, especially genital, difference. The four-year-old boy, as a result of increasing genital awareness, will desire his mother, thus bringing him into potential conflict with a father who is seen and experienced as rivalrous. Fear of paternal retaliation, a consequence of the boy's desire, will add a new dimension to the recognition of anatomical difference. Freud believed that boys notice the absence of a penis in girls, which they suspect to be the result of castration, while girls, recognizing a 'lack' in themselves, become envious of what the man has and by definition contemptuous of their similarity to their mothers. Phallic over-valuation leads the girl to either cling on to the fantasy of being a man – a masculine complex with a consequent disavowal of things feminine – or to renounce in disappointment all things symbolically associated with phallic activity. As a consequence, boys are expected to become associated with traits that are called 'masculine': outer-directed, assertive and potent, while for girls 'femininity' requires them to be 'inner-directed': tentative about themselves as equals and ambivalent about their active participation with the world.

Girls, in the process of turning to their fathers out of disappointment with their mothers, will be exchanging activity for passivity, and in that way becoming father's object. Passivity, being the object of someone else's desire and having no agency of one's own, becomes the hallmark of what is termed 'femininity'. Apart from the possibility that this is socially, as opposed to biologically, determined, the difficulty that Freud had, and that psychoanalysis has struggled with in not 'knowing what women want' was a result of the theoretical difficulty of being able to view women as 'subjects of their own story'. How can objects desire? In education, as elsewhere, 'female passivity' has masked that which has been renounced: desire. In the search for nurture and the demand to nurture others, the woman's desire has been lost. Desire here would include the sense of active agency, aspiration and mastery in relation to academic attainment. Women, in the process of becoming 'feminine' abdicate desire and seek it through the agency of another. Becoming an object of desire deals with the problem of desiring: we may not need to want if we can ensure that we can turn ourselves into something that is wanted.

Mothers and daughters

Post-Freudian accounts of gender differentiation have focused on the earlier stages of infant development. Melanie Klein focused on the girl's early and ambivalent relationship to the mother as being instrumental in the need to turn away from her to the father. The girl is preoccupied with the inside of the mother's body and what it represents in fantasy – be it food, nurture or aspects of what are assumed to be the father, that is, phallic potency. Envy at what it might contain leads to fantasies of damaging and destroying the mother, which, through projection, leaves the little girl anxious about the possibility of retribution, setting the scene for an intensely problematic relationship with the mother.

As Melanie Klein stated (1931):

> My observation . . . (has) led me to recognize the existence of an anxiety, or rather anxiety situation, which is specific for girls and the equivalent of the castration anxiety felt by boys. This anxiety situation culminates in the girl's idea that her mother will destroy her body, abolish its contents and take . . . children out of it . . . It is based upon the child's impulse of aggression against the mother

and her desires, springing from the earlier stage of the Oedipus conflict, to kill her and steal from her.

In order to deal with, and attempt to master, these frightening anxieties the girl turns to a preoccupation with what are culturally designated as 'female concerns': empathy, concern for the other in relationships and, most importantly, an 'inward directedness' which leaves her susceptible to being less concerned with being in, and mastering, the world than boys. Klein highlighted the primary role of the mother which is developmentally more primitive than the Oedipal Freudian father. Thus it may be claimed that she was stressing – as did Freud – the importance, or dominance, of one dyadic relationship over another.

As a result of being the same sex as their daughters, mothers, it is suggested, tend to merge more with their daughters, placing greater emphasis on attachment and relational qualities and making the issue of separation potentially more problematic for their daughters (Chodorow, 1978). Sons, being the 'opposite' of their mothers, tend to evoke a maternal idiom that reinforces separateness and difference from the beginning and are consequently encouraged to be different and to individuate, or enter the world, at a much earlier stage. This framework suggests that in order to develop, boys have to separate from their mothers and identify with their fathers. An implication of this would be that masculinity is always defined as a repudiation of femininity, however that is construed, and as a consequence of that which has been rejected and left behind, 'femininity' or 'womanliness' will always be disparaged or negatively connoted.

There is no developmental necessity or encouragement for girls to do the same: indeed, in this framework it is more likely that girls will be encouraged to resist separation and stay attached to their primary object of both gratification and frustration. Development – that is difference – for girls may involve betraying the mother. If sons are different from their mothers, then there is pressure, psychological and societal, to affirm that difference. Mothers, while nurturing their attachments to their daughters, may feel impelled to assist their sons towards separation. As boys need to transfer their identification from mothers to fathers at an early age, issues of difference and separation are potentially addressed and accommodated to from the beginning. For girls, however, since these issues are not developmentally acute (and frequently there is some pressure for them to be actively denied) issues of separation, including anxiety-provoking fantasies associated with the achievement of autonomy, are potentially more complex and conflictual, and persist into adulthood as doubts about the self. In this model, separation, rather than being a developmental obstacle for the woman, would be a process of continual and conflictual concern throughout her life. Primary maternal preoccupation may apply as much to daughters as to their mothers. Mothers have been, and still are, daughters.

As a result of the early recognition of difference, boys become less preoccupied with the ambiguities and intensity of relational life than their sisters. Clearly there may be some societal and educational reinforcement and advantage for boys in being less occupied with personal relationships. The girl's preoccupation with relational issues of intimacy and empathy may merely equip her for those occupations or tasks defined by society as requiring those frequently gender-specific attributes. The implication of this would seem to be that work, including education, does not become a primary source of self-esteem for women, for whom success and failure in relationships are more important. Greater orientation towards relationships and interdependence would suggest that achievement and success, linked as they are to an idiom of separateness, are potentially more conflictual for female – as opposed to male – identity. If woman's self-esteem is closely associated with being 'emotionally connected' to others, then their developmental goals may differ from those of men, for whom the assertion of difference, autonomy, and independence may be more highly related to their self-esteem, and become developmental aspirations. If women are more preoccupied with being with or doing things for others, unease or guilt may be a consequence of certain forms of success. The 'relational self' may be threatened by education, which involves competition and rivalry and becomes equated with separation, aggression or destruction. A sense of personal 'disconnection' may be the result.

If femininity is equated with a quality of passivity (and ambivalence about maternal separation courts a certain form of submission), then being assertive – or what is culturally defined as assertion – may be seen to be unfeminine. The actively successful woman may not merely alienate (over-valued) men, but court social unpopularity or rejection. There appears to be a greater cultural reinforcement, particularly before adolescence, of dependence and compliance in girls, while independence, self-assertiveness, if not aggression, is (however ambivalently) valued in boys. The 'active pursuit of the myth of one's own passivity' may be, for women, a cultural imperative.

It follows from this that the mother-daughter relationship contains within it a disposition for a problematic ambivalence. Mothers may be both competitive with and fearful of their successful daughters, while daughters may struggle with an identification with their mothers, who are experienced as critical, devalued or unhappy (see Josephine, Chapter 8). Guilt at being different from or surpassing mothers may link with a generationally and culturally reinforced maternal ambivalence about mothering which is simultaneously held in high esteem and denigrated in roughly equal measure. In this sense conflict around a woman's independence and autonomy may be generationally transmitted and in danger of reproducing itself. Social – if not psychological – constructs such as 'motherhood', with its implied submission and renunciation, and 'formal education', with its covert or less-than-covert assumptions about the woman's perceived aptitudes, interests and roles will go some way towards ensuring that 'femininity' reproduces itself. This form of reproduction may apply not only to the choice of subject at university and occupational selection, but also to the decision to choose neither of these and become a 'housewife or mother'; in other words, reproducing the mother's life by an identification with her which deals with the problem of separation by becoming the same. Clearly this form of reproduction operates on a societal level as well: the labour market depends on a substantial number of 'women's jobs'.

The frustrated and hurt girl who turns away from her mother in disappointment towards her father may not need to become an 'honorary man' out of a sense that that is all there is available, but to be rescued from the helplessness implicit in the process of being mothered by a mother who is all-powerful (this would also of course be a strong incentive for boys). This can lead to a split between an identification with an admired father, which for the woman is socially and educationally functional, and an identification with a potentially attacking and devalued mother with whom she is in constant danger of being reunited. This dilemma exists for both men and women in the more explicitly 'feminine' areas of their lives. Thus it is the omnipotent and omniscient mother who is fled from, rather than the powerful compensatory father who is sought. This would apply to both boys and girls, and if the notion of femininity is so defined as to be equated with 'relational' qualities, it may lead to the ambivalent disavowal of everything associated with those qualities.

The initial preoccupation with and implicit over-valuation of the father in psychoanalysis has been followed by a similar attention and over-valuation of the mother. Arguably the same process has occurred in education, where the teacher has moved from being an instructor to being a source of nurture and facilitation. One of the difficulties of this bi-polar model is that while one is dominant, the other's absent existence can only be inferred by reference to the one who is present; it is thus a negative inference. We know what we are by reference to all that the one who is dominant is not. It is as though one must under-function for the other to over-function. If woman functions as man's 'primary other' – that is, an object to his subject – it merely mirrors the dualism that permeates contemporary Western culture (Benjamin, 1990). If we define woman or femininity as all that man or maleness is not, it becomes possible to view the woman as, say, playing nature to man's reason. Male reason (that is, intellect) is set against female nature (that is, unpredictable emotion). We can see in education how the pervasive belief that the latter is in danger of subverting the former leads to a renunciation of all that is associated with what is defined as feminine. To be enslaved (or re-ensnared) by that which is female and which we have struggled to escape from is a fate best forgotten or suppressed.

Separation and independence

If we accept the contention of the previous chapter of the inter-relatedness of subject and object, then the process of gender differentiation will clearly involve, and be the result of, the interaction between various diverse influences. Benjamin (1990) suggests that gender polarity is another form of splitting. What needs to be kept apart are the functions associated with masculinity and femininity. As mothers represent 'the prototype of the undifferentiated object' both sexes will view independence from the mother as a developmental goal: but it is the mother as an object – or concept – which needs to be left, leaving the actual – or subjective – mother unrecognized. As girls 'possess no obvious way of de-identifying from [their] mother[s], no hallmark of separateness ... the feminine tendency is not to emphasize but to underplay independence'. Girls will recognize that maternal strength derives from an idiom of self-sacrifice, becoming both concerned about destroying their mothers through their own independence, and identified via compliance with a version of themselves that is unable to distinguish between what they want and what their mothers want. Boys are able to deny their need for (m)others while girls are persistently in danger of being enmeshed with an (m)other. It is Benjamin's contention that little girls may want the same thing as boys: separation based on difference while maintaining an identificatory link based on similarity. Since it is the father from the beginning who represents the outside world (that is what is different) he will always represent the way into the world. It is the 'father of difference – the "original representative of excitement and otherness" ' – that assists separation. As a consequence boys will have more straightforward access to 'the father of difference' (who simultaneously represents similarity) than girls, for whom separation from the mother is more problematic. Since the father may be viewed by girls as that which she is not, she may be faced with the recognition that a cornerstone of 'masculinity' (equated with being independent and in the world) is the denial of 'femininity', making forms of mastery of the environment, of which educational success can be seen to be one, dependent on a renunciation of that which is defined as 'feminine'.

Separation, and the qualities associated with it, becomes negotiated in the framework of gender. A consequence of splitting will be that the girl will be torn between 'a father of liberation and a mother of dependency . . . to desire (or be the subject of desire) requires a repudiation of the maternal role . . . feminine identity itself'. Women will require men to desire them as a way of de-identifying with their mothers. Becoming an object of male desire aids separation from the mother but leaves the woman without any experience of her own desire or sense of active agency. The choice is between a developmentally progressive father and a regressive mother. Maternal danger is dealt with by paternal rescue. Masculinity is associated with independence while femininity is linked with an enmeshed oneness and dependence. As Benjamin states:

> . . . the father in whatever form always represents difference and enjoys a privileged position above the mother. Her power is identified with early, primitive gratifications that must be renounced, while the father's power is associated with development and growth. His authority is supposed to protect us from irrationality and submission; she lures us into transgression.

The implication is that the father, in representing something outside the self, will be rational and reality-oriented, while mothers will represent an irrationality that may drive us crazy.

These may not be our biological fates but culturally ascribed functions which resonate through our definitions of masculinity/femininity, fathering/mothering, and what it is to be male or female. More often than not it is the man who goes out to work and the woman who stays at home. The construction of femininity or masculinity may occur as a result of the interplay of our anatomical and socially prescribed destinies.

What we make of education may be linked to both our perception of ourselves as male or female (we cannot have it both ways) and the qualities ascribed to the successful adaptation to those roles. For some reason we cannot be allowed or allow ourselves to 'pick and mix'. We may be encouraged to believe that the female physicist and the male nurse are contradictions in terms. It may be argued, in its manner of teaching, selection and assessment that the educational system perceives women only in relation to men. If man is the norm, and we have seen how developmental theory has struggled to free itself of this notion, then women will be judged on the presence or absence of those male qualities deemed to be congruent with educational success. An academic model that defines the task as impersonal, non-emotional, rational, autonomous and values independence and self-sufficiency can hardly be said to be free from socially ascribed notions of gender. Nor can brains that are 'razor sharp' (see Jill in Chapter 8).

Clever girls

'Clever girls' may have to go to some lengths to disguise their active potency. Able or successful women may have to 'put on a mask of womanliness to avert anxiety and retribution feared from the man' (Riviere, 1929). 'Womanliness', for Riviere, 'can be assumed and worn as a mask, both to hide the possession of masculinity and to reverse the reprisals expected if she were found to possess it – much as a thief will turn out his pockets and ask to be searched to prove that he has not the stolen goods.' Women, in the desire for the socially ascribed 'masculine', may need to obtain it surreptitiously, purporting to affect a femininity which is defensive in nature; this deals with both the guilt and fear of retribution as a result of the woman's hubris in desiring that which is deemed masculine.

If a socially constructed patriarchy, which is internalized as a psychological reality by both men and women and reinforced by the effect of the early preoccupation with the enigma of genital definition and functioning, fears the notion of an all-powerful femininity and all it represents, then it needs to be kept under control. One way of doing this is to ensure the threat is ascribed to one sex. Women, needing to choose between femininity and academic success, may internalize the dangers ascribed to their gender and be led to under-function. They may even share society's ambivalence or naked distrust of 'clever girls', and, coupled with any real or imagined maternal envy, resist both taking in knowledge and performing academically. If 'clever girls' threaten men – but also possibly themselves – by becoming 'clever women', one way of dealing with this conflict is to renounce either the 'cleverness' or the 'womanliness'. How can women become educated and retain those socially sanctioned womanly qualities? One way, suggests Riviere, is in her description of a

> ... clever woman, wife and mother, a university lecturer in an abstruse subject which seldom attracts women. When lecturing, not to students but to colleagues, she chooses particularly feminine clothes. Her behaviour on these occasions is also marked by an

inappropriate feature: she becomes flippant and joking, so much that it has caused comment and rebuke. She has to treat the situation of displaying her 'masculinity' to men as a 'game', as something *not real*, as a *joke*. She cannot treat herself and her subject seriously, cannot seriously contemplate herself as on equal terms with men; moreover, the flippant attitude enables some of her sadism to escape, hence the offence it causes.

Women like Jenny may have to choose between becoming clever or sexual. Attempts to combine the two are never straightforward. In order for us to maintain some semblance of gender differentiation women may have to remain 'feminine'; that is passive, submissive and inward-directed, since we may be worried that if women become clever and successful they would become more like men. Melanie Klein in her paper 'The role of the school in the libidinal development of the child' (1923) pointed out that both boys and girls on entering school face the same problem: in order to learn and feel comfortable with their increasing knowledge, they need to 'abandon a passive (feminine) attitude'. This may be more straightforward for boys than for girls. A clever woman must be sexless; intellectual discipline, serious learning, may unsex the female mind. Knowledge and intellectual attainment are women's forbidden fruit; we, both men and women, may be more comfortable with women as Eve – a temptress leading men's minds, if not bodies, astray. Women's desire, in the educational arena, needs to be 'hidden, perverse or acquired by stealth'. In this sense, as Susie Orbach (1993) has pointed out, a woman's feeling of under-nourishment can be experienced as an 'unentitlement', leading to a peculiar form of renunciation and involving a fear of that which is potentially nourishing, be it food or knowledge.

It is not merely in the dynamic of male tutor–female student where this is in danger of being enacted. As we have seen, the extent to which women have internalized these roles – as opposed to having them ascribed to them by men – is the extent to which women's internal saboteur is at work. A female tutor may subconsciously share or believe in the myth of her own passivity or unentitlement, and, feeling devalued herself, project these feelings onto her female student. It is not uncommon to hear female students complaining of the severity, rigour and harshness of their female tutors, who are perceived as betraying a lack of confidence in their abilities (which we may view as the tutor punishing her own feelings of inadequacy by projecting them into the student) while speaking warmly of the tolerant attention from a male tutor whose indulgence may mask a certain contempt.

It was just these issues that brought Polly to consult a counsellor. A graduate mathematician, Polly had reached a stage where she was experiencing herself and her work as unsatisfactory, and suspected that her female supervisor shared her low opinion of herself. She had recently ended a relationship with a man which had been plagued by Polly's vaginismus, leaving her feeling a mixture of guilt, dissatisfaction and relief.

Polly had been brought up by respectable upper-middle-class home county parents, and went to boarding school at age eight. She had always been a high achiever academically, who had developed an awe and respect of analytical intellect. This functioned both to please her when she could 'solve' a problem, but haunt her when, as increasingly often happened, she was made aware of an intellectual deficit in herself by the cleverness of others, who 'strangely, are usually men'.

She was the younger of two able daughters, but had always felt that she was a 'grave disappointment to her parents', particularly her father, who she suspected had wanted a boy as their second child. Polly dealt with this by becoming tomboyish; she climbed trees, became interested in science, and developed a manner of austere disapproval of what she perceived as 'girly qualities'. As a teenager she had become 'fat and bookish' as a way of dealing with sexuality, an option that she viewed, as a young adult, no longer either available or attractive to her. Androgynous and striking in appearance, with cropped, fair hair, her abrasive and distant manner contrasted markedly with moments of acute sensitivity and thoughtfulness.

Adopting an approach to counselling more commonly seen in men – cautious, reserved and apparently self-sufficient, betraying an emotional life ruled by logic, while deeply, almost cynically, disparaging – Polly intermittently showed a curiosity about herself that she experienced as troublesome. Preparing for counselling as she would for a tutorial: marshalling her arguments, working through a pre-prepared list of questions which required answers, Polly was uneasy when, upon the completion of her agenda, she would lapse into silence, having nothing more to say, feeling unable to 'fill up the space' and expecting her counsellor to say something both illuminating and clever, which, when attempted, was met with polite mockery. The consequence was the development of a therapeutic 'vaginismus'. Polly was not going to be prised open. Passivity and silence, problematic qualities for her, were her only defence.

It became apparent that Polly experienced herself as an impostor: a 'phallic' woman who, in her refusal to be penetrated by either

her boyfriend or counselling, was guarding against any acknowledgement that she was a woman, much as she had done (out of a belief that her father would approve) throughout her childhood. Better to remain a tomboy avoiding penetration, although Polly was clearly intruiged by the possibilities that being a woman might offer. She needed to protect herself, but against what or who? Her idealization of the intellect – often described by her as 'piercing' – was at the cost of something else.

Polly would often appear pale and anaemic, and what little she ate was described as 'junk'. Little danger, then, of taking in or of being impregnated by something of value which might form the basis of a certain form of attachment. An over-valuation of an intellect that could be penetrated (or penetrating) and pierced (or piercing) dealt with any doubt about whether Polly wished her body to be infringed. Minds can be penetrating, that is, 'male', but bodies must not be penetrated, that is, 'female'. Polly knew she wanted to be a woman but was unimpressed with all available definitions of femininity, based as they were on a renunciation of things 'masculine'. In her confusion about whether she was desirous or ugly she nurtured a quiet self-disgust at her self and her sex, while her secret and subjective collusion with her father to become his tomboy, although leading to a feeling of hollow triumph, left Polly estranged from herself and nursing an uncomfortable feeling of dislocation.

Polly's difficulty with her work, which was becoming increasingly complex, had led her to a 'block' which prevented her from being 'able to think any further'. Mathematical curiosity was becoming a violation. Others, her clever peers and colleagues, and her counsellor, could be curious, but Polly was unable to allow herself to think cogently about herself, others or her subject. The tragedy was that Polly was by nature a curious person for whom the issue of an ascribed and confusing gender was preventing her from being able to think further about her science. The more she thought about herself as a woman, a topic that was taking up an increasing and unwelcome amount of time, the less she was able to hold on to her intrusive and penetrating curiosity. In relationships a wish to submit co-existed with a refusal to do so pointing at the absurdity of having to do one or the other.

The demand in education, as elsewhere, for gender polarity (that is, having to choose between traits which are seen as mutually contradictory) can be viewed as one major reason why both men and women struggle from time to time with the educational task which requires the student to be both intermittently active and passive, submissive and dominant, intuitive and logical. The issue may be less about the 'difference between the sexes', but more about the dilemma that both face between needing and wanting. Splitting of gender traits enables us to believe that we have been able to circumvent this problem by turning one sex into an object which desires and the other into its subject which needs. If competition, assertiveness or aggression (deemed to be 'male') threaten the concept of relatedness (deemed to be 'female'), then these parts may be projected into the other, enabling the woman to rid herself of traits that are defined as problematic for her, while men may jettison the more relational parts of themselves and either denigrate, mock or revere them in the woman. Either way we stay in touch with that which we have been encouraged to renounce. The problem is that what makes us feel real and alive is the unwillingness of the other to accept our projections.

Arguably an educational system whose organization, process, and content reinforces the belief in gender polarity will leave the student in danger of feeling one-dimensional and flawed. The construction of something called 'masculinity' and something called 'femininity', and the necessity of having to choose between the two, denies and negates the importance of recognizing sexual and gender interdependence. Learning and creativity may be about discovering similarities and opposites in the other, but also within oneself.

Benjamin contends that development consists in the search for mutual recognition. That is, if our formative experiences are about being together or separate, then we will constantly be searching for forms of recognition (that which makes us feel real), where we will need to continually tease out the enigma of being like someone else and being different, or distinct, from them. The discomfort, if not pain, that this implies leads via the mechanism of splitting to the belief that each gender can only recognize one aspect of the self. Being the same as and being distinct are split apart and placed into gender. Splitting into subject/object, good/bad, doer/done to becomes a way of avoiding what Benjamin calls the 'difficulty of dealing with the contradictory tendencies within the self', and when placed in gender become the prototypes of various forms of domination and submission. An 'intersubjective perspective' which recognizes the importance of the discovery of difference and similarity as a developmental necessity for the infant, as well as acknowledging the importance of the interrelationship between self and other in the construction of the emerging personality, may go some way to negating the need to split our environments into objects and subjects.

While education may explicitly or implicitly demand and confront both sexes with the necessity for gender accommodation along the lines suggested, psychoanalysis may teach us that resistance to sexually ascribed roles and divisions flourishes not least in neurotic symptoms and the errors of everyday life. In that way the unconscious does its work. The unease with gender polarity for both men and women may result in the simultaneous defiance of and submission to choices which appear mutually exclusive and potentially depleting. A girl who is as good at science as the best of the boys at school who then chooses to read English at university – which she then under-performs at – may have made the choice on the basis of gender determination rather than academic ability, but may also be enacting a protest at the tyranny of gender polarity. The female student who does not talk in tutorials in the face of her outspoken male peers may be enacting a refusal to comply in a manner which is actively disdainful, rather than passively overwhelmed or inhibited.

Normative accounts of the generational transmission of 'femininity', 'mothering', or even 'sexuality' only lead to explanations of 'normative' behaviour. Psychoanalysis would suggest that unconscious sabotage may lead to the unconscious transmission of something quite other from the official version. Subverting the educational self may be one way that women simultaneously comply and reject maternal injunctions. Arguably, later in life it is theoretically possible to renegotiate behaviour and attitudes ascribed to one's gender, but it is in education, more particularly as an adolescent at school, that the consequences of gender polarity are both most in evidence and in danger of being significantly reinforced. Education may contribute to and influence for good or ill the process and outcome of the struggle that boys have to become men and girls experience in the conflict to become women.

In this chapter I have attempted to tease out how qualities that are perceived to be 'masculine' or 'feminine' are constructed and the relative values attributed to them in education. These may determine the nature of the educational obstacles for both men and women. Femininity and masculinity are constructs which are socially ascribed and differ according to their specific context. In the following chapter I shall be looking at the context of contemporary education and discussing some of the possible psychological obstacles which may result.

7
Commodities

Just as the student does not exist in a vacuum, neither do institutes of higher education. In this chapter we shall look at how educational institutions reflect, or attempt to meet and adapt to, social requirements or demands, and how this may affect the individual student. Educational institutions have evolved to meet social needs or agendas and are affected by how society defines the purpose of education at any given time. Education constantly interacts with a wider society whose norms, goals and culture are constantly changing, which will influence the process of learning and teaching.

Many of the processes that we have been describing in relation to the student and the experience of learning are likely to be replicated by the institution and be instrumental in enabling – or hindering – learning and growth. Just as student unease may be linked to relationships between people, rather than intrinsic to the individual student, the student's developing relationship with the institution will affect the process of learning. Students may have transferences to the institution, and to the concept of learning, while institutions may develop certain counter-transferences to their students and the processes of learning and teaching.

People will have different forms of transference expectations towards higher education depending on their previous experience of institutions or their functions. The combination, as we have already seen, of nurture, judgement, competition and selection inherent in education will ensure that many students will view their institutions of higher education in ways similar to the way they viewed those structures which have previously carried out comparable functions. Institutions may offer developmental hope or despair. Just as people develop 'parents in mind' – as third-party points of reference – students also have the potential to, in anticipation, construct a 'university in mind'. Through splitting and projection these may become benignly helpful or malignly persecutory. Equally, educational institutions may welcome students as potential partners in the pursuit of knowledge, or view them as a source of disruptive irritation which must be managed and controlled.

The institution as container

The emotional experience of being part of an institution (and how it is used) will be a result of the interaction between the individual and the institution. Exclusive preoccupation with individual symptoms of unease or failure carry the danger of obscuring the role of the institution in creating, maintaining and reinforcing the symptom. The inability or unwillingness to learn or to be educated is unlikely to be solely located in the individual student. It is reflected in the complicity of the educational institution and the wider society in defining both the nature of education and who is to be educated and how this should occur. An individual's ambivalence about certain forms of learning and knowledge may be shared by the institution. The institution may project this onto the student, which then becomes formulated as the student's difficulty to study and function. The pursuit of knowledge, or the definition of what is to be taught and how, can be defined by the institution in a manner which makes it problematic for certain students to adapt and flourish. Educational institutions may define, or be forced by their paymasters to specify, what modes of thought or thinking are acceptable, and in that sense facilitate or hinder the capacity for 'mature thought' as opposed to the forms of 'non-thought' described by Bion. Institutions, like primary caretakers, might have to be containers for impulsive thought or action, which have the potential to be metabolized into creative thinking.

Some problems of learning or adaptation to education may be iatrogenic, that is, caused, defined, and reinforced by the institution. The question is then raised: would this student have this problem or symptom if they were not at this institution? Students may be vulnerable to certain forms of developmental stresses, but whether these will be translated into symptoms will be dependent on the specific response and nature of the educational establishment:

> Celia was a young 17-year-old woman recently arrived at university, having never before been away from home for any extended period. For the first two weeks she felt tearful and lost, and was often seen crying and alone on campus. Her tutor became understandably concerned about Celia's evident distress and her difficulty working, suggesting to Celia that she see the college counsellor. The tutor's agitation led her to phone the counsellor in advance of Celia's appointment, explaining her concern with the words that she 'was worried that Celia might do something silly', although what was not specified. The tutor thought Celia was so distressed that she ought to return home.
>
> While self-harm or suicide was not mentioned, it became apparent that Celia came from a hall of residence where there had been a student suicide recently which had been dealt with rather clinically, without much acknowledgement or discussion. On meeting her counsellor, Celia's first words were, 'My tutor thinks

I'm going to kill myself because another student did last term. But I'm not; I just feel lonely and lost and my tutor's worry is making me more upset.'

Individual pastoral help may pathologize the student for institutional problems or anxieties which are outside the student's control. The extent to which institutions are sensitive to these issues may be in some measure dependent on the clarity of their goals and structures. This raises the question of the purpose of education. Is education classically liberal in the dispassionate search for knowledge as an end in itself, engaged in a form of social engineering, a device for social or occupational selection, or merely engaged in the certification process for certain forms of (un)employment? It may also have some form of custodial, rather than explicitly educational, function. Increasing numbers of young people going into further education can be viewed as a way of dealing with unemployment and thus a form of applied social policy, if not control.

With these multifarious and unclear goals, educational establishments may be forgiven for being perplexed about their tasks and function, and just like individuals need to develop routines and rituals, if not defences, to deal with the anxiety aroused by this unpredictability and confusion. Difficulties within educational institutions may be linked with the relative failure of the wider society to define coherently and consequently carry out the primary task of education. Even when some form of clarity of purpose is achieved, educational institutions can function with two sets of contradictory structures uneasily co-existing; one formal, rational with clearly demarcated responsibilities and roles, while the other is informal, private but discernible, and more dependent on the personal relationships that develop between individuals. We are again confronted by the split between one structure that is explicit, rational and cerebral while the other is more diffuse, reliant on the emotions, and consequently seen as being irrational and unpredictable.

A central feature about educational institutions is that they often involve periods of constant transition. Transition involves greater potential dependency on the part of the student, while being faced, initially at least, with greater unpredictability in the responses of others who the student may be ambivalently dependent on. This may lead to uncertainty as to the appropriate way to behave or approach the task of studying. Tutors and institutions will have to face and manage their own reaction to being confronted with students struggling with these issues. The structures that are evolved to deal with this may involve the form of coping or defence mechanisms that can provide short-term alleviation of the immediate stress, but lead to longer-term harm. This has similarities to the infant having to create some form of order and security out of a situation which is both chaotic and confusing, as we have seen in Chapter 1. In establishing a system that acts against current anxiety (both personal and institutional), mechanisms of splitting and projection may be used which lead to institutional practices which impair the functioning and performance of both the institution and its members.

Defensive structures

Isabel Menzies-Lyth's (1988, 1989) pioneering work in this area was predominantly focused on describing nursing and residential settings for children, but her description of the defence mechanisms operative in these institutions to ward off anxiety, and their unintended dysfunctional consequences, are no less relevant to educational settings. In pointing out how a rigid splitting of roles in nursing functions to deny the relatedness between nurse and patient, she was also suggesting how institutions need to be aware that the complexities ensuing from the recognition that people are interdependent and share an at times difficult and confusing relationship need to be regulated and managed. Menzies-Lyth suggests that these defences may deal with the latent anxiety, but a too-rigid demarcation will rapidly become impersonal and dysfunctional, leading to a sense of personal dissatisfaction and disempowerment in both nurse and patient. Similar analogies can be seen in education, where the institution's dealings with, and management of, both staff and students is concerned.

Ways in which this process happens may include the negation of individuality through categorization and depersonalization, where 'blanket decisions are made or allotted to categories of people' which involve a 'rigid and inflexible' enforcement of methods of standardization. All students are then inducted and assessed in a similar fashion, regardless of their individual characteristics or needs. The difficulty here is that if education is essentially made up of people (teachers, students, administrators, etc.) who 'are the instruments of technology', then, as Menzies-Lyth points out, 'the instrument cannot be standardized.' The detachment and denial of anything associated with feelings or emotions deals with the need to minimize interaction that might lead to forms of attachment; the demise of the individual tutorial relationship or small-group teaching may be an unintended consequence of this. Decisions – that is, discretional use of personal initiative and thought – are kept to a minimum by rigid descriptions of 'task performance' (affecting both student and tutor) and a 'purposeful obscurity is maintained in relation to formal responsibility' (the fledgling student spends a great deal of the first term trying to ascertain who is responsible for what within the institution and the tutorial relationship).

These function to deal with issues of anxiety, guilt, doubt and uncertainty in a situation that is always changing, and thus contain in more than one sense the possibility of a benign response to the confusion associated with being part of an institution. The difficulty occurs if these mechanisms or 'solutions' function to mask and deny recognition to the very real anxieties they represent. We have seen how the infant is enticed to negate elements of its disturbing reality through a form of hallucinatory denial, and needs to find ways of managing its adaptation to the environment in a way that recognizes the nature of its real existence without it becoming overwhelming. Institutions may need to do the same.

Splitting

Excessive splitting and projective mechanisms in the service of denial can lead both infants and universities into harmful ways of relating to themselves and the outside world. Splitting in infancy universally functions to dissipate anxiety as a result of the frightening experience of being an infant in relation to an unpredictable caretaker or world, but is always in danger of preventing the infant from confronting the nature and source of his anxious concern. It is a way of denying the reality of the situations we face, thus paradoxically increasing a dissociated unease akin to Bion's 'nameless dread', which leaves us less able to master that which is frightening. Institutions and infants need to know the true nature of what they are up against if they are to grow and develop. As Menzies-Lyth states, a university that 'facilitates . . . the evasion of anxiety but contributes little to its modification and reduction' will always be in danger of encouraging, if not forcing, the student into 'a maturational level (and way of functioning and behaving) below that which they had achieved before becoming . . . [a student]'. This may involve functioning at the developmentally primitive level of incorporation, that is sameness, rather than at a stage or process which recognizes difference and autonomy.

Narcissism

Membership of an educational institution will have some effect on the behaviour and personality of its members. This can be influenced by identification (if you cannot identify with the institution you are likely to be rejected or 'find membership too stressful and leave') and introjection (an acceptance and personal accommodation to its norms, values, ways of operating and 'received truths'). What form of identification or introjection is required of students in contemporary educational establishments? If universities are in danger of using developmentally primitive psychological mechanisms in dealing with anxiety resulting from society's ambivalence about their role and function, then does it follow that students too, confused as they are about what script they should be addressing in higher education, will grasp at more rudimentary and thus psychologically unhealthy coping mechanisms? Since subjective experience and cultural conditions and pressures are inextricably intertwined, it is not unreasonable to assume some reciprocal link and interchange between the two.

Gerry was a 27-year-old graduate student who appeared for counselling at a stage in his studies when he had amassed a great deal of material but was unable to put pen to paper. What was most striking was both his appearance and his manner. Although born in South America, Gerry gave the singular impression of being an Englishman *manqué*: brogues, tweed jacket, waistcoat and pipe were complemented by an impeccable Oxbridge accent. Speaking at length without making himself understood (which seemed to be the academic problem), Gerry explained that he and others saw himself as being 'exceptional' in his field, and that on completion of his doctorate he had been promised a number of prestigious positions both in industry and in the academic world. He had worked hard and deserved these accolades, since he had done everything required of him, including constructing a C.V. which impressed even him!

His past, which he had ablated in his desire to become an Englishman, seemed to Gerry to have no meaning. An only child and a 'mother's boy', who had 'endured' a difficult relationship with his father, 'an uncouth philistine', who he held in utmost contempt, Gerry had become a clubbable Englishman in an attempt to escape being a foreigner (and its association with difference) and to acquiesce to what he felt was necessary for contemporary success. Desperate to fit in, he combined an ingratiating manner with a thinly veiled contempt for all those standing in his way, who were thought to challenge his 'exceptionality'.

Despite his verbosity there was something profoundly unresponsive, frozen and inhibited about him, preoccupied as he was with the effect he was having on the other. Self-absorbed and rather disinterested in others, he would become mockingly dismissive of anyone who did not share his own opinion of himself or the world.

Not writing, but having done an enormous amount of research, that is, knowing it all, was a way of not only preventing himself becoming known to others, but also protecting his own version of himself as exceptional: if he were to set pen to paper, others would judge him and may find him wanting, which would lead Gerry to have to recognize both others as different and the ordinary aspects of himself.

Beneath his assumed servility, Gerry was contemptuous of those who sat 'in judgement' over him. Part of him felt that he should be awarded his doctorate without having to go through the process of writing a thesis; others should recognize that they had a prodigious talent on their hands – it was an 'outrage' that he should be asked to write. Having to write, and court not being 'exceptional', would mean symbolically leaving his mother, the 'light of whose life' he was, and take his chance in a world both outside his immediate control and whose demands were unpredictable and in essence unreasonable. For supervisors, all elderly and childless, Gerry functioned as something special. They radiated unreserved approval of Gerry's ability; but for that to continue he would have to write, which, paradoxically, carried the threat of his downfall. Gerry's narcissism prevented him from engaging in the process of learning. His fantasies of grandiosity, self-sufficiency, and omnipotence clashed with his need for others. He had constructed a self which he felt others would want and be impressed by, while turning himself into something that was thought to be 'marketable' and in demand.

A culture, educational or otherwise, which extols the self at the cost of the relational, will always be in danger of leading us back to an illusory self-sufficiency and insulation which seeks to deny our relatedness to others. Education may reinforce narcissistic 'solutions' which, while offering spurious fantasies of comfort, protection and self-sufficiency, in essence involve a retreat from the world and its complexities and a denial of the relational. Students, preoccupied with issues of narcissism – that is, with versions of who and what they are and can be – need to be able to establish a link between self-preoccupation and their relationship with others. To be encouraged to experiment with this may be an important function of the student's learning. This applies not only to adolescent students, of course. As Bion (1967) says: 'The problem for the psychoanalytic human is the resolution of the conflict between narcissism and social(ism).'

Cultural factors will in part define the outcome of the oscillation between selves which are experienced as intermittently omnipotent and denigrated. Society and education may reinforce a 'culture of narcissism' (Lasch, 1979), which extols an excessively isolated self-preoccupation to the exclusion of concern for others. Other people are then experienced as extensions of the individual self; separateness is negated since others are not experienced as different or distinctive in their own right. What follows is either an omnipotent over-valuation of the self with associated contempt for others, or a passively dependent idealization of and accommodation to others, with an accompanying self-contempt. There is no link between the two states of mind, and any frustration is dealt with by explosive or silent outrage. The narcissist, as Bollas has pointed out, 'doesn't just look into the mirror but assumes the other to be the mirror'. Education would then be required to reflect back a form of self-love which, both in its denial of difference and the fantasy of it being under our control, would become a form of 'masturbatory gratification'.

Since narcissistic states of mind demand constant self-affirmation and obedience, they require the negation of either others or the self, leaving us vulnerable to humiliation, denigration, or contempt. The rapidity of cultural change and the versions offered by contemporary education that everything, and nothing, is within our individual grasp, may reinforce a tendency to retreat into a form of insulation where everything new or different is a potential threat and needs to be guarded against. A climate of self-interest is created with minimal tolerance of difference which is antithetical for real, as opposed to synthetic, learning to take place. Curiosity and pleasure in learning is eclipsed in favour of a hollow compliance and the demand to become 'marketable'. If narcissistic solutions are choices we make in response to the trauma of our environments (Symington, 1993), they are potentially reversible, and it would follow that educational institutions – and society's definition of what an education is for – have the capacity to determine, or even prescribe, what form of personal solution we are encouraged to adopt.

Consuming education

In a culture that values end results more than process, students may need or be encouraged to turn themselves into products in the belief that in becoming a commodity they are making themselves more marketable. Education may then become a way of packaging ourselves in a form that society understands and espouses. If education is viewed and marketed as a commodity, then students as consumers are buying something that may or may not be of value. Education, unlike other consumer durables, does not come with a guarantee. Education as an investment (involving some form of acquiescent renunciation in the hope of a postponed future gratification), involves the danger that the rewards may not be found to be commensurate with the sacrifices made. If we are encouraged to turn ourselves into commodities at no small cost to our psychological integrity, then we may find ourselves bewildered and enraged when in turn we are not 'bought'. Having purchased via education a ready-made identity involving the dutiful acquisition of information, rather than the capacity to think, we may be required to deny aspects of ourselves which involve doubt and contradiction.

As Lasch (1984) has pointed out, turning oneself into a commodity involves the distillation of ourselves into a minimal or shrunken self which has to survive at all costs. The minimal self, preoccupied with a form of one-dimensional survival based on what we assume or are led to believe is demanded of us in order to succeed, becomes inevitably preoccupied with narcissistic insulation, where spontaneity, contradiction, and playful curiosity are eliminated. Imaginative creativity may give way to blandly packaging ourselves to the demands of the environment. The links with a shallow and one-dimensional false-self development are self-evident. Students who are encouraged to aggressively market themselves may be selling a product that is all packaging and no content. Learning becomes something that must be endured: a means to an end product.

Turning oneself into a commodity involving, as it must, issues of insulation and safety, inevitably leads to '. . . [the] drive to be normal . . . [a] numbing and eventual erasure of subjectivity in favour of a self that is conceived as a material object among other manmade products in the object world.' Bollas terms this 'normotic illness', an interesting description with its suggestion of a socially transmitted infectious disease, where the primary symptom is an abnormal need to be normal. While a predisposition may be set in infancy, with the parents 'deflecting the child's subjectivity into material objects', cultural reinforcement will be instrumental in attempts to turn our subjective selves into material objects.

Fromm's dictum of 'the more you have the less you are' in an educational context becomes 'we are what we achieve' via qualifications, C.V.s or examination success. The process involved in the search for 'normosis' involves the projection of the internal world and all its ambiguity onto a material object, say education, enabling the person to 'use' and 'collect' objects (i.e. qualifications), which, since they 'serve no symbolic function . . . have no meaning'. The outcome is 'meaningless plenty'. Facts 'can be collected, stored and possessed', which, since facts have little subjective meaning, can be a reassuring activity in itself. Since the normotic person does not see himself as a subject, 'he does not ask to be seen as such by the other, nor does he look into the other' as a subjective being. He exists as an object in a world of objects which are there to be mastered or accommodated to; subjectivity and difference are alien concepts.

The student as commodity

Developmentally, Bollas sees the constuction of the normotic personality in terms of a mirroring deficiency in the family, where the infant is only partially 'seen' or acknowledged as a subjective being by the parents. The consequence is a certain 'homeostasis or shutting down on life' where the goal is a state of 'inorganic constancy'. Just as parents may 'refuse to acknowledge the child's inner subjective reality', so too can the tutor. Education may demand a normotic response from both its students and teachers. The normotic person welcomes being part of an institution 'because it enables him to be identified with the life or the existence of the impersonal; the workings of an institution ... part of a team, at home in a committee ... secure in social groups that offer psuedo-intimacy [as] an alternative to getting to know someone.'

The student is praised and rewarded, often materially, for being good, that is ordinary, and 'adapting to convention', while ignored or threatened for being imaginative or different. Equally, the tutor may be encouraged to relate to the student as a commodity which has to be processed and managed.

This was an issue deliberated at the discussions of the Vienna Psychoanalytic Society in 1910:

> [Teachers] have no time because a constantly expanding curriculum has to be mastered ... as a result ... teaching is becoming a chase, and the teacher is never free from anxiety ... the teacher who should direct himself to the student as a whole, tends to disappear behind the mere educational technician. Since he has no time for the individual, he begins to work more and more with that abstraction 'the class'. His natural ambition is to achieve a high standard with 'his' class. When he finds a slow pupil resists his attempts to carry him along he soon begins to feel an understandable desire to get rid of the boy before he 'lowers the general level'. (VPS, 1910)

Seen in this light, dropping out or truancy assume a different complexion. In the same paper, Karl Monitor comments on the relationship between education and society.

> It is not the educational system that creates these pressures, but the

role society calls the school to play . . . our educational system is only secondarily educational; it is primarily an institution for the attainment of privileges. . . . the important thing is not how the individual develops during this period but what he achieves . . . the teacher is turned into an instrument for social selection.

As a consequence, education becomes a 'hollow framework to be used for material reward, with the student and teacher accommodating to a structure set by others'. The normotic 'flees from dream life, subjective states of mind, imaginative living, and aggressive, differentiated play with the other', and, in the quest for normality, is driven further from experiencing himself as three-dimensional. Again, to quote Bollas:

If the psychotic has gone off the deep end, the normotic has gone off at the shallow end . . . The most fragile period in a normotic person's life is during adolescence. It is my view that we can often observe how a child raised in such an atmosphere feels unbearable strain and turns to either drugs or suicide as an alternative to life in the family. We can also witness the family dynamic more clearly, as normotic parents often exorcise themselves of their adolescent child as if they are cleaning the house.

Normotic functioning becomes another defence against thinking subjective thoughts. Education then becomes less of a process (that is, a dynamic and interactional relationship) than something that is 'swallowed whole for its material benefits' and consequently static and one-dimensional.

A culture which sees education as being involved in the business of objectifying certain forms of normality, rather than encouraging difference and diversity, will breed unease; the urge, and demand, to be normal nurtures a seething discontent. An educational culture which is normotic in its orientation will lead its students to value the functional and material rewards that education may bring as long as these rewards are not threatened or that there is no 'demand on the subjective self'. We may be able at some cost to turn ourselves into commodities, but resent being left on the shelf or any evidence of ourselves as subjective beings:

William was an intense and focused young student, who consulted a counsellor specializing in work and study-related problems since he appeared to have difficulty managing his work effectively. He had always had a 'foolproof' way of approaching his studies involving detailed and highly structured schedules and meticulously worked out timetables. Having treated studying as a 'not very enjoyable but necessary job', he was finding it increasingly difficult to stay 'on top' of his work, and thought he needed expert help on study techniques. William spent his sessions with his counsellor devising ever more intricate study programmes, lists of things to do and how to do them, and discussing the technical aspects of the use of textbooks and how to read more quickly, all with little or no apparent success.

After a couple of meetings, William, looking increasingly pale and haggard, apologized to his counsellor that he would not be able to come to his next session since, unbeknown to the counsellor and hitherto unmentioned by William, he had to attend his father's funeral. William's much-loved father had died shortly before William made contact with the counsellor. Was it possible to reschedule the next day since there was an aspect of essay writing which William particularly wanted to discuss with her?

The student who merely seeks study skills, in order to 'get back on the rails' as quickly as possible, at a time in his life of major emotional upheaval, may be struggling with the difficulty of continuing as a commodity in the face of evidence of a subjective self which cannot easily be packaged. Learning – as opposed to education – is, as we have seen, less of a material transaction than a process of personal transformation. The danger is when formal education turns the pleasure in learning into a material commodity, where knowledge and learning can be converted into social success and material wealth provided we become objects.

Increasing concentration of power and production, the growth of diffuse and anonymous organizations, and a culture which demands conformity and marketability may require both narcissistic and normotic states of mind and behaviour of its students. Higher education, as an Eriksonian 'psychosocial moratorium', where students can experiment with their own subjectivity in the context of some degree of protection from the outside and objective world and 'do their growing up while they were students', now appears to be under threat. Arguably, students are expected to enter higher education fully grown up; to know who they are, what they want, and how to get it. The construction of an impressive C.V. for those equipped to do so has become a pedagogic imperative.

Freud (1909) suggested that the task of education, was to '. . . enable the individual to take part in culture with the smallest possible loss of individual energy or originality'. A prescient recognition that the two might be difficult to integrate. A culture that encourages or duplicates the conditions that give rise to narcissistic modes of thought and operation in the lives of individuals (in being confused, confusing, and demanding excessive and one-dimensional compliance and adaptation) will foster solipsistic solutions in its citizens. These may involve a withdrawal into the self, excessive dependence on others as objects for self-esteem, and require a way of relating to others as material commodities. The problem is that education like development is about frustration. Just as adolescent narcissism requires a challenging and sustaining presence and authority to liberate the adolescent from the terror of his own omnipotence, thus enabling him to enter the world as it and he is, so too education is inevitably frustrating in requiring us to recognize our own limitations and defer certain pleasures:

> Education is the preparation of the child for adult life. We persuade ourselves that if we give the child 'a beautiful childhood' we give him a store of memories rich enough to last him the rest of his life. We forget that an ear made sensitive to pure harmonies can be all the more grievously upset by any sudden disharmony, and that the finest effects can be secured by dissolving disharmonious chords. Every educator who encourages a child to forgo a pleasure is on a higher ethical plane than one who leads him from pleasure to pleasure (Wilhelm Stekel in VPS, 1910).

In this sense, education as a means of combating our own narcissism will inevitably prove bewildering and enraging for the narcissist.

The purpose of education

Part of the problem is the difficulty society has with the concept of education. Is education an end in itself, or a means to other material ends? Are students being educated for life, or for a particular strata of society? While education has traditionally transmitted a relatively consistent culture and traditional skills to its students, contemporary society, confused as a result of the increasingly rapid and fragmentary technological changes that it is struggling to control, has looked towards education to contain if not resolve some of the associated difficulties. Education, while still being asked to have a primary function in the generational transmission of a cultural heritage, which is increasingly becoming fragmented and unclear, is also being asked to function as an agency of social reform and change.

The need to teach 'skills' to enable people to take their place in the labour market conflicts with education's function of enabling young people to experiment with what kind of adults they want to become. Education, in needing to 'teach' how to work and how to play, is constantly being asked by society to do one or the other. Attempts to do both are viewed with suspicion, despite the fact that the two are intertwined. After all, you have to go to school to use the playground. This was a point made by Illich (1971), who raises the interesting dilemma of the distinction between what someone should be taught and what we want to learn and whether 'instruction', including the demand for objective measurement, can ever be imaginative.

As education has moved to become a form of social engineering as well as selection, with its emphasis on head-start programmes and targeting the 'disadvantaged', classrooms and lecture theatres have become nurture playgrounds. This may be developmentally appropriate if we view trust and safety as prerequisites for learning, but it augments a trend towards teachers becoming substitute (including better or compensatory) parents which has reinforced a confusion about the educational task, not least manifest in the split between state and independent schooling. Education as a form of social engineering has always appeared problematic; no less so than psychological engineering or psychoanalytic determinism.

It is never quite clear whether formal education involves a benign wish to socialize the young or a need to control and master that which we do not understand or have forgotten, and find threatening. Does education protect youth or colonize them? When adolescence is viewed as potentially dangerous, disturbing, or destructive we may require formal education to control that which challenges our accepted truths. We may be excused for wishing to rein in the challenging, direct, and subversive nature of the young student and reassure ourselves that they are or will become just like us. In assuming that we are, in requiring the young to be educated, curing them of their more problematic behaviours, we may in effect be reassuring ourselves that our own uncomfortable and possibly destabilizing attitudes and feelings are being dealt with by proxy. What other explanation, says Illich, could there be for '. . . the social decision to allocate educational resources . . . to those citizens who have outgrown the extraordinary learning capacity of their first four years, and have not arrived at the height of their self-motivated learning . . . [this] will in retrospect probably appear bizarre.'

If education is essentially about the eventual acquisition of qualifications or skills, and the involvement in and the engagement with a culture which nurtures, protects, and facilitates personal development, then these two aims need to be complimentory. The danger is in assuming that the former will inevitably lead to the latter, rather than recognizing that the latter enables the former to occur and flourish. If the decision to become a student might increasingly be a negative one – an escape from the lack of employment possibilities or the assumed problems in becoming an adult – then it would be unfortunate if these 'refugees from a hostile environment' were fleeing to an illusory sanctuary. Just as the therapeutic setting of psychotherapy needs to offer a balance between sanctuary and challenge – a breathing space for thinking and feeling to occur – so too, optimally, should education. The emphasis on coercion or moralistic 'shoulds' in both education and psychotherapy will ensure that both cease to have the capacity to be pleasurable. When we lose touch with our desires, what we want or would like, under the onslaught of what others tell us we need, something of importance is lost in the inevitable transformation, only to continue its existence in our subjective and often secret worlds:

> The school must never forget that it has to deal with immature individuals who cannot be denied a right to linger at certain stages of development and even at certain disagreeable ones. The school must not take on itself the inexorable character of life: it must not seek to be more than a *game* of life (Sigmund Freud in VPS, 1910).

In the next chapter we shall address the question of what may happen when education, or more specifically academic attainment, takes on the character of life itself.

8
Cleverness

. . . clever beyond hope is the inventive craft he possesses.
It brings him now to ill, now to good (Sophocles, 'Antigone').

When true knowledge proves irrelevant, one is free to invent (Javier Marias, *All Souls*, 1989).

An extremely depressed but able student referred herself to her university's counselling service with the words, 'The worst thing about being clever is that you can never be clever enough.' This was a curious statement: the implication being that cleverness is somehow infinite, and consequently something to which one can aspire, safely located in the elusive but wished for future. The seemingly implicit assumption in her statement was that we might, could, or should be able to attain the state of 'clever enoughness' which may in part, as a consequence of its cultural over-valuation, be a form of 'holy grail' sought by many of our students. In this context it becomes a curious form of self-tyranny which may well distract students from other aspects of their personal development, and reinforces the split, which as we have seen is so pervasive in education, between intellect and emotions. This split is often enacted in higher education by the distinction (and frequent tension) between the counselling or medical services, which are seen to represent or speak to the world of the emotions, and the academic, teaching or tutorial functions of the institution which are equated with the intellect. Possible friction which results is often on the basis of mutually disowned projections. It is short step from there to view intellectual and emotional development as two totally separate activities in which it is often assumed if not accepted and expected that the latter has to be sacrificed to the former:

Catherine, the seeker after 'clever enoughness', was a young 19 year old who found separation from her close, rural family extremely difficult. As the eldest and brightest of the children she spent her childhood helping to look after the younger children and being clever at school. This seemed to her a reasonable compromise, but she always felt at some level that while looking after others and being clever was enough, something was missing. She took great pains not to be too clever at the local school for fear of isolation from her peers. She had few friends – other children seemed to appear suspicious of her cleverness as, she felt, were her family. However, being clever was an identity she reluctantly came to accept, as it seemed to deal with and explain why she had so few friends, suffered from unaccountable mood swings, and had never had a boyfriend.

At university she was confronted with the problem that other people were just as if not more clever than her, but they also appeared to have both boyfriends and a social life. Cleverness seemed acceptable, in fact you could not get enough of it, but Catherine could no longer hide behind being clever as a compensation for what she felt were social and emotional deficits. Her subject was English, and she was a gifted student. Her particular interest was literary deconstruction, involving 'taking things apart to discover their true meaning'. One evening she was writing an essay on the subject when she was struck by the thought that 'there is nothing there in the text'. She was found sometime later wandering aimlessly around the town muttering to herself and taken to her doctor.

This late-adolescent woman had deconstructed herself; as with the text she had peered into an abyss that was her own internal world and personal life, which had provoked a breakdown, which, in terms of her emotional life, needed to happen. Her fear that if everything was stripped from her cerebral attainments there would be nothing left had led to a realization that behind her somewhat precarious intellectual development lay a host of unaddressed issues from early childhood.

Intellectual cure?

In education, breakdowns can be breakthroughs. An additional complication for Catherine was that others, including boys, had to be protected from her intellect. This category also included her mother, who had spent her life as a child-minder and in consequence was perceived by Catherine as a person of nurture rather than intellect who needed to be protected from Catherine's 'cleverness'. Cleverness, or academic attainment, can be used for myriad purposes. Often, as with Catherine it can be used as a refuge from personal lives which feel too problematic.

The difficulty comes when there is nowhere left to hide. It is possible that conflictual issues which we thought we had dealt with prior to puberty by becoming clever or successful at school return to haunt us when our cleverness is challenged, or its perceived benefits begin to be experienced as illusory or shallow. What we had repressed in the playground returns with a vengeance in halls of residence and lecture theatres. Could it be that higher education forces us to face problems that we thought we had dealt with when we were younger by becoming academically successful? This could include separation, compliance and conflicts around the nature and function of both social relationships and academic success. What this suggests is a classic example of the return of the repressed in psychoanalytic theory where what we have attempted to forget returns in a disguised and displaced form. We may attempt to use our intellects to cure those parts of ourselves which are experienced as too vulnerable or dangerous. We can think of or know everything as a way of experiencing nothing. Intellectual performance can be the student's attempt at a self-cure. Masud Khan has suggested that in psychoanalysis the most difficult thing to 'cure' is the patient's attempt at self-cure, and it may well be that in education what is most problematc to renounce is the demand on oneself to be clever, especially if it is associated with a developmental foreclosure. An adolescent corollary of this is the belief that we can control our bodies with our minds. Catherine's mind was sharp, lean and incisive, while her experience of her body was of a physical presence that was flabby, gross and unfocused. An alternative attempted solution would be to control our minds, which are experienced as over-active and full, if not sadistic, with our bodies. Examples of this would include certain forms of promiscuity and drug abuse in highly able and gifted young people.

Childhood traumas or slights may lead us to embrace premature and precocious intellectual development and achievement, '... not realizing we may be replacing one tyranny for another'. In 'Infantile neurosis as a false self organization' Khan (1974) talks of a student who, as a result of a premature separation from his parents, develops an obsessive attitude to education and intellectual attainment, in the belief that if he becomes the 'best' student his parents would return to him. Our intellectual selves can become creative inventions – if not fictions – designed to deal with past trauma. If we experience our childhood selves as empty, bereft, or lacking we might be tempted to deal with this by becoming 'precociously full, even better if we can convince ourselves that others envy our fullness'. The difficulty here arises that if our cleverness or academic success is dominated by a need for us to feel 'full' while others are 'empty', which is dependent on arousing envy in the other, others are required to reciprocate by parading their inadequacy and envying our brilliance. If that is not forthcoming – or they are unwilling to cooperate with this subjective script – the project iself, academic success, may appear both hollow and pointless.

If being clever carries with it the possibility of circumventing certain developmental problems, it is always in danger of leading to a form of obsessive asceticism which can be experienced as both one-dimensional and brittle, since our cleverness is located in only one part of ourselves. The sacrifices it requires may be welcomed as a way of dealing with potential pleasures which feel too difficult. When we become aware of these potential pleasures – that is, what we are missing – and our need to renounce them, or when we realize that we can never be 'clever enough' and that the attempt to be so is a psychological chimera, we are always in danger of imploding on ourselves. In higher education the dangers of elevating academic success to the point where it is directly equated with a person's intrinsic worth are self-evident. Arguably, thinking is essentially an aid in trying to remember what it is we really want. The risk is when cleverness becomes divorced from one's own curiosity and preoccupations. A self that is clever stands apart and encapsulated from a self that is secretly something else. Being clever then becomes a defence against finding out what we want; it has only tenuous links with learning, play, experimentation, or pleasure.

John Stuart Mill's extraordinary education has become a kind of fable of pedagogic ambition and of the way a parental demand can structure a child's life. Taught exclusively by his father, and having no contact with other children apart from his own siblings who he had to teach, Mill started learning Greek when he was three and Latin when he was eight. Between the ages of eight and twelve he learnt 'elementary geometry and algebra thoroughly, the differential calculus and other portions of the higher mathematics'. As well as reading at this time a good deal of the most important classical literature, he also wrote a history of the Roman government. At 12 he began learning logic and when he was 13 his father gave him what he calls 'a complete course in political economy'. Mill concludes, 'I started I may fairly say, with an advantage of a quarter of a century over my contemporaries.' That is to say, by the age of 15 Mill had the learning of a man in his late 30s; the experiment was, as Isaiah Berlin has written '. . . an appalling success' (Phillips, 1994). Phillips goes on to suggest that Mills' breakdown in young adulthood was a protest against the life his father had organized for him and a consequence of an over-valuation of intellectual achievement at the expense of a certain form of pleasurable thoughtfulness.

True and false selves

Winnicott (1965) describes a form of personality organization in which there exists a false self, which is essentially in danger of becoming hollow and adaptive, and a true self, which has the capacity to be spontaneous and authentic. In people for whom there is a high degree of split between the true and false selves there is the danger of a certain form of psychological impoverishment particularly if the true and false selves come to represent a psychic split between the intellect and the emotions:

> A particular danger arises out of the not infrequent tie up between the intellectual approach and the false self ... when a false self becomes organized in an individual who has high intellectual potential there is a very strong tendency for the mind to become the location of the false self, and in this case there develops a dissociation between intellectual activity and psychological (somatic) existence ... When there has taken place a double abnormality 1) the false self organized to hide the true self and 2) an attempt on the part of the individual to solve a personal problem by the use of a fine intellect, a clinical picture results which is peculiar in that it very easily deceives. The world may observe academic success of a high degree and may find it hard to believe in the very real distress of the individual concerned who feels phony the more he or she is successful. When such individuals destroy themselves in one way or another instead of fulfilling promise, this invariably produces a sense of shock in those who have developed high hopes of the individual.

Winnicott alerts us to the possibility that our intellects may be colonized by something profoundly inauthentic and alien, which, as a threat to the integrity of the self, will need to be continually subverted while at the same time most vigorously pursued. The depletion of the self can be the result of relentless over-valuation of the mind at the cost of distrust and avoidance of our emotions. Cleverness or academic success as an end in itself may be associated with the part of ourselves which we consciously most value since it has certain social and cultural advantages, yet from which we feel most estranged. In education one of the questions we need to ask ourselves is, 'What developmental issue is this person avoiding by being or becoming clever?'

In psychoanalytic theory the difficulty in approaching this question is that development itself may be infused with concepts of success and failure. Psychoanalytic developmental theory is a progression – we know when we are doing well – which raises the possibility that both education and psychoanalysis share similar dangers. Both may be addictive and encourage the search for and development of false-self solutions to what is experienced as personally problematic.

The false self is essentially adaptive and compliant, geared as it is to the avoidance of difference and the relentless necessity to seek out sameness. The true self is more concerned with exploring conditions where a more authentic and spontaneous articulation of the self is both possible and encouraged. It is thus primarily about difference. Reciprocity may be an ideal paradigm of the early mother-infant relationship, but should the mother be experienced as intrusively demanding by the infant – and it is difficult to think of a form of parenting which is not experienced as exacting from time to time – a precocious compliance is nurtured in the infant which seeks to both manage the mother and adapt to the environment as it subjectively exists. With this development a false self is constructed. This may appear and intermittently be experienced as real and as a functional way of managing the world. Simultaneously a true self – consisting in part of all that is not adaptive, compliant or conformist – is secretly nurtured, forever seeking out conditions for its recognition. These conditions may include the need to undermine and sabotage the false self, which has come to represent a response to a reality which is both intrusive and demands something of us which we are reluctant to give. The construction of the false self is by definition closely associated with a certain developmental foreclosure which restricts curiosity and the possibility to think creatively about our desires independently of external impingement.

> . . . if the mother impinges on the infant with her own desire and so does not allow him the opportunity for illusion, he can only comply with her in order to survive. For Winnicott it will be his notion of the false self that will be used by the child to manage the burden of the imposed illusion that is not his own; the child . . . 'presents a shop window or turned out half' [to the world] (Phillips, 1988).

The false self demands that spontaneity and desire be suppressed in order to obtain love and safety. For Winnicott, the false self always '. . . lacks something . . . and that something is the essential element of creative originality' which may be innate in infancy, but is either fostered or hindered through the process of mothering and our experience of being parented. Our own experience of 'aliveness' therefore becomes an achievement and cannot be taken for granted. The false self, associated with compliance and adaptation, will always be in danger of courting futility, emptiness and despair without us ever being aware of the source of our unease. It is the distinction between feeling real and having reality ascribed to one by another and consequently always being dependent on the other for a certain form of recognition. In this it is closely associated with the problem of whose needs are being met – or allowed to be recognized – in the mothering couple. If we look in the mirror and only see another – or another's needs – then the possibility of us experiencing ourselves as truly real – and capable of an authentic spontaneity – is severely limited. For Winnicott, the infant's spontaneous gestures are precursors of a true self, which, if unrecognized or negated, forces the true self into hiding. The hiding place is the false self, which ensures that the true self can subsequently only be inferred by referring to all that the false self is not.

Not infrequently, through a failure of nurture, the false self comes to represent notions of self-sufficiency, competence and invulnerability. Its relationship to the true self, like the Trojan Horse, ensures that the false self (in its desire to protect the true self from being discovered) will always be threatened by that which it is seeking to protect. It is perhaps not surprising that it is in relation to academic success, and the uses to which our intellectual capabilities are put, that this conflict – stemming as it does from an aesthetic of parenting – becomes most acute, particularly where the false self is closely associated with academic attainment or certain subjective uses of 'cleverness':

Josephine was a very clever girl, but the cleverer and more academically successful she became, the more anxious she got. Matters came to a head a few months before her A-levels when she became tearful and morose, complaining of insomnia, nightmares and a terror of being unsuccessful in her attempt to get into university, which 'would be the end of my world'. Her teachers were surprised and concerned as Josephine was the one pupil in the school who was thought certain to obtain a university place.

Josephine was the elder and more academically able of two sisters. Her father was a successful academic, while her mother was an equally successful, if secretly denigrated by Josephine, housewife. She had always been top of her class, and university had been her goal for as long as she could remember. She aspired to an identification with her professor-father, while fearing what would happen should she not get into university or, what was even worse (truly unthinkable), some of her less-able friends succeed, while she did not. She took great satisfaction from her academic success, but could never relax. Her only other source of concern was a worry that her sister was not doing terribly well at school and that this much-loved sibling might be psychologically impoverished as a result. The problem with one's intellect being unconsciously associated with one's own sadism and ruthlessness which needs to be defended against will be discussed below. The aspect of Josephine's fear of failure that may have been associated with a problematic feminine identification – she secretly thought of herself as 'the pudding' and thought her mother must be depressed as a consequence of 'not having a proper job.'

Her nightmares consisted of her classmates gloating at her failure and of Josephine being chased naked through the school. In her friendships it was of extreme importance to surround herself with others who were as clever or cleverer than herself, or with people who were seen as extremely successful in other fields, be they sporting or romantic. She sought friendships with people who 'were better' than her and whose function was to make her feel inadequate, which however uncomfortable was preferable to being friends with anyone who wanted to get to know her, which by definition, meant they were less able and consequently not worth knowing. The result was that she rarely felt at one with herself, a contempt which was masked by a veiled snobbery.

Much of her waking life was spent in an internal dialogue with herself which went as follows: If she worked hard and got into university it would only be because she worked hard; if she worked hard and did not get in, it was because she was not clever enough and a confirmation of a subjectively held truth; if she did not work and did not get in, it was proof that she was not innately clever enough. The only way to solve this riddle – and prove to herself that her academic competence was not false or illusory – was not to work and then be accepted by the college of her choice, a risk of course that she could not allow herself to consciously take for fear of being discovered as an emperor without any clothes. However, because her anxiety was such as to prevent her doing any satisfactory work, she was effectively embarking on the one course of action calculated to make her more agitated.

What eventually transpired was that what Josephine consciously experienced as a fear of failure was the representation of an unconsciously veiled hope: it was only by not getting into university that her true self – that part of her, of which she felt only dimly aware, which contained the capacity to be truly creative, authentic, and not at the mercy of external and internal persecutors – could establish the conditions for its emergence. The fear that she might not get in was in effect a fear that she might 'succeed' in doing so, thus an unconscious hope. Getting to university would in effect abandon her to the continuation of her false self existence, which, while outwardly successful, meant that Josephine never felt either adequate or substantively whole. Intellect and academic success were solely correlated with her false self, which in itself reflected an idiom of parenting and led to Josephine constantly fearing yet wishing for another self to be recognized, leading her true self to continually seek pathways towards recognition. Achievement may betray; the symptom tells the truth.

> In the healthy individual who has a compliant aspect of the self but who exists and is a creative and spontaneous being, there is at the same time a capacity for the use of symbols . . . By contrast, where there is a high degree of split between the true self and the false self, there is found a poor capacity for using symbols, and a poverty of cultural living. Instead of cultural pursuits one observes in such persons extreme restlessness, an inability to concentrate, and a need to collect impingements from external reality so that the living time of the individual can be filled up by reactions to these impingements (Winnicott, 1965).

It is not uncommon for highly intelligent or well-respected and successful people to secretly nurture a nameless dread which defies all rational explanation and exerts an almost compulsive if not fatal attraction. Conscious anxiety about further 'success' – which can be experienced as a particular form of depletion – masks a hope that the true self, which can only be experienced as the antithesis of the false self, will find a way of asserting itself even though the way may be objectively viewed as destructive or harmful to the individual.

In education, a highly organized false self, while appearing very successful, may in effect be antithetical to real learning as it is associated with a rigidity of the personality as a result of it being essentially a defensive construct. That is, knowledge becomes an illusory defence against our own helplessness, vulnerability, and need for others. The compliant and adaptive self, brought into existence at best to deal with external reality and at worst to ward off psychological chaos by accepting and accommodating to the control of others, has to renounce exploration, assertion, and the recognition of separateness which true learning and feeling psychically alive involves. What becomes particularly problematic is when the false self sets itself up as the true self and it is mistakenly assumed that that is the real person. Helene Deutsch (1965) first commented on the 'as if' personality which lacks authenticity and imitates the behaviours and attitudes of others, which can lead to them making '. . . good pupils, compliant (and) adaptable but lacking originality and creativity'. We can fool ourselves and others and behave 'as if' we are learning – learning itself can then become an 'as if' activity; experienced as both unreal and corrosive.

The false self – aside from its benign function as an adaptation to the environment – can be a prematurely precocious way of mastering what has been experienced as a childhood trauma. Our intellectual selves can be seen as inventions to deal with trauma. When the false self is synonymous with the mind or intellect it can become a way of forgetting, and by that mastering, our emotional selves. A brilliant mind stands in front of a vulnerable or frightened psyche. The mind then stands in danger of taking itself as object rather than something which is subjectively perceived. The mind takes responsibility for an environmental failure. It becomes a refuge, somewhat apart or dissociated from our experience of ourselves as real, where we can shelter from any unease stemming from the human environment. It is less a part of us than something almost external to us that we cling to when we want to forget that which is emotionally problematic. A consuming, obsessive attachment to intellectual achievement is frequently the result, which, when eroticized can be difficult to relinquish. It can also lead us to learning the wrong thing:

> ... through puberty and adolescence such (false self) persons experience little that enlarges or enriches them, and live shut in an unreal world of their own concoction. It is this that alienates them not only from others but themselves as well ... however the price is high in their unease with others (and their) overvigilant self-protective alienation from their human environment (Khan, 1974).

Rolf was a 32-year-old graduate student who, after three years spent on his thesis, was nowhere near completion. He procrastinated endlessly, had little respect for his supervisor who he believed was his intellectual inferior and consequently had little to offer him, and spent much of his time going to dinner parties and attending prestigious social events. He cultivated the appearance and demeanour of an eligible bachelor: well groomed, charming, and affable. His family were excessively proud of both his academic success and his undoubted social ease and competence, and Rolf believed that one of his great virtues was his ability to get on with 'people from all walks of life', remaining courteous and amenable even in the most trying of circumstances, such as the 'unacceptable and inappropriate' demands his reviled supervisor was making of him.

It became apparent that his parents had always wanted him to be bright and charming, and had rarely if ever acknowledged any disagreement within the family or any reason why Rolf should feel angry or resentful. The problems with his supervisor were clearly making Rolf's characteristic ways of dealing with these situations – by latent denial, compliance or social seduction – difficult. Rolf felt enraged but had no suitable vehicle for its expression. He dealt with his resentment towards his supervisor by becoming over-amenable, thinking that his supervisor would then be placated and see things Rolf's way.

Rolf had spent most of his life charming and ingratiating himself with others and had in return received positive confirmation that he was well liked. He had become increasingly aware that his social graces effectively enabled him to control the response of others. The price he paid seemed to Rolf rather reasonable: a modest amount of conformity in attending to the perceived needs of others at the cost of an intermittent lack of spontaneity in creative thought both about his subject and about himself. The strategy was clearly not working with his supervisor, which left withholding any work from this 'demanding and insensitive man' Rolf's only way of making himself known to his supervisor and himself. Rolf was profoundly ambivalent about his own capacity to function potently. Assertion was to be avoided at all costs as it courted difference; he 'massaged' people (in his spare time Rolf worked as a masseuse) as a way of ensuring that any negative feelings were not expressed. However, his problems with his supervisor left him feeling 'cross', recognizing a part of him that wished to be 'naughty'; something which in his childhood was not acceptable. His version of himself as self-sufficient and autonomous was equated with an escape from those that wanted something of him, but resulted in Rolf feeling he always knew best. Through his polite and mannered behaviour others would not impinge: how could they if he was giving them what he assumed they wanted? Interestingly, Rolf once claimed that he had 'toilet trained myself because I couldn't bear being fussed over'. This, however, left him with a problem with his assertive, or different, self.

He was beginning to experience a muted sense of anger but was unable to make any sense of this sensation. He needed to emasculate himself, but at what cost? In this sense his diplomacy might be self-defeating. At one point while ridiculing his supervisor Rolf spoke about having learnt nothing from him academically: 'the only thing I have learnt at this unversity is how to behave at dinner parties and be diplomatic', which, as he was becoming increasingly aware, was just what he needed to unlearn. He needed to learn the art of misbehaving, or at least thinking about what he might want and ways of getting that through the assertion of difference. Compliantly learning how to behave and learning how to be well liked, if not respected, had replaced real learning and experience for Rolf, who increasingly felt unreal and depersonalized in his over-vigilant attempts to appease the other.

Safety, predictability, and continuity can be achieved through intellectual aspirations – or over-functioning – but at the cost of our inner lives feeling constantly lifeless, shallow, and under threat. In education we are always in danger of learning something which can be metabolized in psychologically malign ways. Conversely, getting or doing things wrong may involve a secret pleasure more real than any successful achievement:

> On my first day [at school] I demonstrated my total lack of understanding through a rejection, which in part still continues, of the [school] system. This is what happened. In response to the command, 'And now take your blotting paper', I immediately complied by pressing with all my strength on the first letters I had just written. It was the right move. But curiously, instead of being absorbed, the fresh ink spread over the lined paper: the sheets of blotting paper were kept inside an exercise book; I had blotted with the cardboard cover. This mistake, which was to be followed by many more, filled me with joy instead of mortifying me. I would attend ... school, since I had to, but I wouldn't be one of the school's pupils. Thus, via my shapeless ink stains a combination was taking shape, in which I recognize myself, of compliance and distance with regard to institutions (Pontalis, 1993).

Moments of failure may connote 'moments of health'. While we may aspire to being 'clever enough' as a way of denying or negating our emotional selves and anticipating living in some unspecified illusory future when we may believe without any psychological conviction that we will have accumulated enough cleverness, we may also come to distrust or be wary of our intellects or academic potential. The fear of our brains and what successful use of them may lead to can, as Josephine discovered, lead to a feeling of apprehensive suspicion towards our attainments. The question arises: who has been damaged by our intellectual precocity?

> Jill was an attractive and extremely bright 23-year-old post-graduate student who, after having obtained the top first class degree in her year was awarded a prestigious scholarship. Behind her vivacious and impressive exterior lurked a young woman prone to unaccountable depressions, who would often become phobic of social gatherings, and unable to share her academic triumphs with friends or family.
>   It transpired that her elder brother had suffered for some years from a severe psychiatric illness which had necessitated hospitalization on a number of occasions when he would threaten violence towards members of his family including, and especially, Jill. On

the last occasion her parents had asked her to leave home as Jill's presence there was by their account exacerbating her brother's condition. Jill had always suspected that her success – more specifically, her cleverness – was disapproved of by her parents, and was seen by them to be negatively influencing the course of her brother's illness. Consequently, she adopted a stance of uneasy ambivalence towards her brainpower and its achievements, which took the form of finding it extremely difficult to 'cope with other people's jealousy of my achievements'. Getting her work published in a prestigious journal led to Jill ensuring that copies of the journal were mysteriously unavailable in her department and that none of her friends were told, Jill going to great lengths to prevent them finding out. Neither her parents nor her brother had been to university, and with her most intimate friends Jill had attempted to cultivate a shell around herself, unable to trust others for fear of an unspecified and vague sense of imminent betrayal.

Jill unconsciously felt that her brains were lethal; they had literally driven her brother mad. Jill perceived her intellect as something autonomous and separate from herself, over which she had little or no control. Ordinary rivalrous feelings towards her brother became fused with the possibility – probability, given her brother's illness – that she had the capacity to destroy him. Her gifts had to be shrouded in secrecy lest they seriously damage others. Jill's anxiety over the jealousy of others can in this light be seen as her fear of a retaliatory attack resulting from the damage inflicted by her for merely being clever. The more successful she became the more anxious she got. What became apparent was the split in Jill's functioning between the successful young academic woman and the confused and panic-stricken girl whose internal world was continually preoccupied with fears of her own capacity for murderous destruction, and of being attacked by others for something she could not help: being clever.

For Jill, her academic career had the potential for driving people mad. The fear is that if we can take pleasure in our brains it can only be at someone else's expense and humiliation. If that is so, and we are led to distrust our innate intellect or curiosity because it is unconsciously equated with our capacity for sadism or voyeurism, then it may be preferable to become benignly stupid rather than malignly clever. We may then be invited to under-function, in which case our capacity for masochism rescues us from our potential for ruthlessness. How comfortable we feel with our academic – or other – capabilities may depend in no small measure on how comfortable we are with our capacity to be, and experience ourselves, as ruthless. As a result, unlike Jill, who experienced her intellect as outside her effective control, others may go to great lengths to attempt to control their cleverness.

The function of failure

We have seen in the discussion of adolescence and the student role that reasons for failing – or underfunctioning – are numerous and often associated with the specific nature of the developmental demands of young adulthood. Failure may result from an inability to master the work, a preoccupation with other, more meaningful, subjective scripts, or an explicit rejection of what is demanded of us. Failure, as Freud pointed out when writing about unconscious guilt, can involve a determined attempt to prevent oneself succeeding out of a sense of guilt at leaving someone behind who has not achieved. Jill may well have taken that route had her intellect felt more under her control. The obverse of Jill would be the graduate student who did feel in control of his brains, and after a successful undergraduate and graduate career stopped working immediately prior to his examinations for his master's degree out of a sense that he had done all he could to court paternal approval through being successful that he would now attempt to obtain at least paternal attention via failing. Failing may be an unconscious ambition, just as dropping out of education may be a way of dealing with uncertain feelings around attachment by a refusal to continue being attached. Students who continue with their studies, failing time after time, may need to cling on to something innately frustrating, or to repeatedly rework something that has been left unresolved.

However, if academic success forces us to face our own capacity for triumph, if not benign ruthlessness, then academic under-functioning may well speak to our potential for masochistic suffering. The skill of the masochist is to manipulate others in order to get sadistically attacked. Thus, not handing in assignments or behaving in such a way as to court dismissal from the institution, would invite a response which tests our capacity to get pleasure out of pain. Other explanations for intellectual inhibitions seek to explain academic under-functioning in terms of a primary ambivalence of the exploring, plundering, or robbing qualities inherent in the search or desire for knowledge. As Melanie Klein suggested, discovery involves the use of a penetrating curiosity. For Klein, the search for knowledge always involves the danger of a violation which invites retaliation; entering the mother's body and securing knowledge may place curiosity into a framework of aggressive plunder, and we may need to make reparation as a way of forestalling the 'inevitable' counter-attack. Knowledge in this sense, like the inside of the Kleinian mother's body, becomes a substance which can be abused (Klein, 1923, 1931).

Is being clever, then, a solution or a problem? The concept of being clever – or having specific skills which set us apart from others – appears in our culture to offer specific advantages and be highly prized. Until fairly recently it has been possible to avoid conscription by the skilful use of brain power, and we seem to have accepted again until recently that students should not need to be held financially responsible for their education. However, this apparent social reinforcement of the benefits of being clever masks a profound ambivalence in our attitude to those with 'brain power'. The social disapproval of those who have avoided serving in the armed forces and the culture of denigration of 'pampered' students betray our mixture of awe and distrust of those who would seek to be cleverer or more skilful than us. As a culture we are willing to tolerate and afford privileges in the name of cleverness, but only if we can concurrently mock and denigrate those whom we reward.

Constructive thinking

Equally, psychoanalysis betrays a fundamental ambivalence about intellect and its vicissitudes. In attempting to combine a theoretical infrastructure which is intellectually demanding with a clinical application which stresses the importance of the emotions, psycho-analysis has become suspicious of intellect and emphasizes 'process' and 'lived-in experience'. Intellect in therapeutic circles is viewed with the same wariness and suspicion as emotion is in educational ones. It is as though intellect, 'braininess', is confused and almost used interchangeably with intellectualization, which is viewed as a malign resistance in any therapeutic endeavour. Just as tutors may need to tease out the emotions behind the brilliant brain, therapists may need to respect the capacity to use one's intellect in the service of the psyche. While intellectualization may be a reflection of our need to deny an emotional truth and a wish for a form of exhibition rather than communication, intellect may enable us to comprehend some-thing about our emotional lives in a manner which may be speedily metabolized. If, as we have seen with both Catherine and Josephine, being clever allows us to circumvent certain developmental issues leading to psychological foreclosure, then it may also enable us to leapfrog others not merely in lecture theatres but also in consulting rooms. There must after all be certain advantages in putting two and two together. The use of intellect may not merely be a defence but also a potentially constructive force in thinking creatively about oneself. In that sense our own stupidity – and the fact that we may always be stupid enough – becomes questionable; it may be that we become stupid when we don't want to understand, or where understanding would cause anxiety, guilt or depression. Obtuseness may allow us to avoid certain trains of thought and ensure that the capacity to make links is undermined.

As so often in this field, it is as though we need to preserve a form of Cartesian dualism. There is something safely reassuring about keeping intellect and emotions split, as though we would not be able to cope with the idea of one being infused with the other. Opposites in this sense may function to stop us thinking. Perhaps we need a defence against ideas of completeness – something always needs to remind us of our limitations. Do we dare disturb the universe by aspiring to be complete – fully three-dimensional – or, say, cleverer than Freud? Psychoanalysis itself struggles to integrate this split: the experiential learning through a 'training analysis', and intellectual learning through the training institution at times merely serves to reinforce and legitimize this dualism. The distinction between knowing and experiencing (and that one defends against the other) is a fundamental tenet of psychoanalysis, thus difficult to relinquish. If you know and feel there might be little to work through.

Completion may imply 'the end' or something finite like death. In common with our culture developmentally we are profoundly ambivalent about knowledge; not having any carries with it the danger of low self-esteem or provoking envy of others who have more, while having too much may deplete and estrange us from other parts of ourselves or lives. An attempted solution to this dilemma is to see cerebral knowledge as something innate and given, while our internal worlds/emotional lives are something totally other, often to be held in contempt or viewed with wary distrust. In this sense part of the problem which is encouraged by, among others, the educational system, is the implicit assumption of the division between work and play, as though there is a weekday self and a weekend self, and that one is simply a relief from the other. A split is then encouraged between weekends when we do not need to think and weekdays when we do.

This split is not merely a function of the external circumstances of our lives. It can also be evident in how we think of ourselves:

> Julian was an introspective and severe young man who had come to university to read science. He had always been successfully competitive, but was troubled by intermittent depressions when he would lose interest in his subject and begin to become preoccupied with matters of an existential nature. Science, of whose truth he

was convinced when feeling well, provided no relief when he was depressed. He secretly envied his fellow arts students, who appeared to be able to 'express and commune with their true natures', which Julian always felt was elusively outside his grasp.

His father, whom he admired from afar, was a successful government scientist who had conveyed to his son the folly of pursuing any other path than that of scientific enquiry. Julian was never fully convinced of the truth of this proposition, especially as his father appeared, to Julian at least, deficient in so many other areas of his life. His father seemed irascible, querulous, unworldly, socially inept, and ill-at-ease with people. A paternal brother had killed himself after attempting to follow a similar career. Julian's mother, in contrast, was floridly artistic, socially sought after to the extent of having had a number of affairs, and expressed a comfort and pleasure with her emotional life, which to Julian appeared both an indictment of his austere father and by implication himself. She was a talented musician, a part of her which Julian allowed himself to emulate by spending all his non-scientific time playing in the university's orchestra, which he anxiously enjoyed.

He disliked the superficiality of most relationships and the hedonistic quality of what he saw as student life, yet on acquiring a girlfriend – a fine-art student – was made aware of the attractions of a life freed from the rigours of scientific enquiry. During his depressions he was plagued by the belief that science was a cause of all society's ills – a force of evil – and he would find himself thinking about escaping to India to meditate, where he would be free to engage in a life of contemplation and artistic creativity.

Julian had split his parental identifications and loyalties between a scientific father and an artistic mother, who were then propelled into representing different parts of himself. He had agonized over whether to read arts or sciences at university, fearing that he could not combine the two, and that by choosing one he would lose touch with the other and all that it had come to represent in his internal world. By choosing science was he condemning himself to a life like his father – and uncle – and rejecting the part of him that was more like his mother, or if he studied arts would he run the risk of betraying all that his father represented and all that Julian himself held dear both about the importance of scientific method and the logical and concise part of himself? Within this conundrum was a deeper and gender-related dilemma: for Julian, to be a man was to be like his father, but to be a person he had to be more like his mother.

Splits may be culturally sanctioned, and educationally reinforced, but psychologically problematic. Having to choose risks losing something we might value. Choosing to study mathematics does not rid us of what studying English might represent in our minds. The 'cleverer' we are the more choice exists and the more problematic this form of renunciation may become.

Education in its search for 'cleverness' is always in danger of diminishing us, while psychoanalysis, in its quest for emotional truth, risks denying us the pleasures of our intellects. While we cannot ever be 'clever enough', in the educational search to be so we are always in danger of setting up ideals which may humiliate us. In this search how can students and their teachers avoid a specific form of self-contempt or reproach which is a short step from becoming contemptuous of others? Catherine and Josephine had sought to be 'clever enough', but in that search something was lost which needed to be rediscovered and reclaimed.

By attempting to split the emotions from the intellect we are attempting to convince ourselves that the two are mutually incompatible and opposite; we are forced to choose where on this continuum we wish to place ourselves or be placed by others. This is a curious dichotomy, since the way we perceive an idea is relatively neutral; for it to become meaningful and of interest to us it has to be invested by us with some emotional meaning which evokes our curiosity. Having to choose between two options may leave neither very attractive. Alternatively, two options may not be enough and serve only to limit our aspirations: we may need more in order to fully do justice to the complexities of our natures.

These issues are highlighted by examinations, which in some form remain the cornerstone of our educational system. It is in the demand to sit and pass examinations that our options are frequently percieved as too limited.

In Chapter 9 the issue of examinations and what they have come to symbolically represent is addressed.

9
Examinations

Everyone fears they are a joke which other people will one day get (Martin Amis, 1981).

My experience of the final stage of education was exactly like that of everyone else – constant worry and sleepless nights for the sake of a painful and useless test of the memory, superficial cramming, and all real interest in learning crowded out by the nightmare of examination, I wrote an astronomical dissertation for the gold medal, and the silver medal was awarded to me. I am sure that I should not be able now to understand what I wrote then, and that it was worth its weight – *in silver*. I have sometimes dreamt since that I was a student preparing for examination; I thought in horror how much I had forgotten and how certain I was to fail, and then I woke up, to rejoice with all my heart that the sea and much else lay between me and my university, and that no one would ever examine me again or venture to place me at the bottom of the list (Herzen, 1994).

While Herzen's subsequent life was marked by imprisonment, exile, and the deaths of his wife and son, it was his period at university, and more specifically taking examinations, which filled him with horror. In spite of this, and the fact that Herzen spoke in favour of institutional reform in various fields, he did not advocate any change to the examination system.

It is a pyrrhic triumph to pass an examination; to be truly memorable, others must fail. What other explanation can there be for the establishment and for the enduring nature of an examination system based upon ensuring the success of the few at the expense of the many? The pleasure in passing an examination, and its anticipated rewards, depends in no small measure on others' failing and being excluded from whatever privilege the successful completion of the examination may hold. If examinations are some form of initiation, then they need to prepare us for the possibility that success is intrinsically bound with some form of exclusivity, while failure remains the preserve of the majority.

Examinations are a continual reminder that there is a first and last, a top and a bottom, and that there is a demand that we take our place in relation to being better or worse than others. Examinations function as early indicators, telling us that this is what achievement is about and ensuring that the acquisition of skills and knowledge are placed, in the framework of an essentially evaluative personal competence, involving issues about where we place ourselves, or are placed, in relation to others. Learning and knowledge which are capable of being examined thus become intrinsically linked with issues to do with competition, rivalry, envy, grandiosity, denigration and contempt.

This would go some way to explaining why examinations are so difficult to relinquish; despite repeated attempts to do away with examinations, they are still with us. In an increasingly secular and technological society which is experiencing the de-integration of family or community networks, examinations often appear as both a sanctuary, something familiar and stable, and as a trusted rite of passage. However, they also speak to something deep in our personal or collective psyches which reinforces the often spurious notion of 'the test'; both its desirability and inevitability. We need to be judged, preferably by an external object, if only to be found wanting. In a personal sense this places examinations in the context of wholeness or fragmentation. To pass may enable us to feel complete, while failure courts the possibility of our feeling disturbingly flawed or fragmented. There is something deeply troublesome about failure and rejection. Success, however, despite its sense of pleasure and achievement, brings with it the danger of a certain complacent satisfaction, which can lead to both a denigration of others, who can safely be seen as failures, and a particular subjective experience of fraudulence. The fear is that the more we have, the more can be taken away.

Examinations, despite the delusional quality of our attempts to pretend otherwise, are more than simple tests of either academic ability or our capacity to function under pressure. As rites of passage they will inevitably come to represent the sum total of our anxieties about both transition and development. Developmental anxiety is never far from examination anxiety. The pervasiveness of minds, as well as bodies, 'going blank' in examinations may be a way of ensuring that we get the best of both worlds: the worst happens – we fail – and the best happens – we do not pass and stay the same.

> Donald was a brilliant student who had done extremely well in his course work, and was set after three years' solid work and achievement to pass his final examinations with a first class degree. After turning over his examination script he found, as a result of the sudden onset of double vision, that he could not read the questions and could not think; his 'brain had become empty', and he began to feel increasingly nauseous. He was a much-adored and pampered child, with an older brother who, although not having

had a university education, had become both wealthy and successful in the world of business, as well as having children of his own
who Donald's parents doted on. Donald only had his academic
success as the source of achievement and parental approval, and felt
ill-equipped to manage so successfully in any other arena outside
education. It was only in his final examinations the reality of what
success would confront him with bore down on him and he became
unable to think and progress.

The academic arena may well be regressively gratifying, but examinations, and more particularly Finals, remind us that this is not an open-
ended option for us. We are faced with a double bind: if success courts
a certain sense of failure, then in failure we may find ourselves
succeeding in a secretly nurtured project. If we succeed we are forced
in some measure to leave the academic institution, end our period of
adolescent dependency, and take stock of ourselves in the adult world.
There is something inherently final about this. Leaving can also
unconsciously be experienced as rejection: we may succeed in our task
of passing the examination, but feel hollow, alone, and abandoned by
our teachers, the institution, and the educational process. If this is so,
then examinations will evoke memories, conscious or otherwise, of
earlier periods when similar emotions were experienced.

Given that examinations are a concentrated period when we are
asked to produce something from within ourselves which is not
regurgitated, we are inevitably confronted with the question of
whether whatever it is we have in ourselves is good enough. What is it
that we have in ourselves that others may want, or conversely, what
part of that which is in us do we want, or can we allow, others to see?
Something that was in some sense given to us now has to be given
back, preferably in a slightly different form. Is it still there or has it
been lost or destroyed? Is what is there ours, or has it been stolen? If
we experience knowledge to be examined as something which has
been obtained through theft (textbooks or teachers who have been
plundered) we may not feel entirely comfortable about giving it back.
If we fear our internal worlds consist of confusion and disorganiza-
tion, will we be able to communicate our thoughts in a comprehensible fashion, 'under examination conditions'? To be judged invites the
danger of being found wanting and inadequate, which can in some
senses be experienced as a criticism both of oneself and one's internal
world.

When we sit examinations we delegate, frequently to an outside
agency, the power to sit in judgement over us. Despite or perhaps
because the examiners are as a rule unknown to us, we can project onto
them the anxiety of our choice. We can have transferences to

examinations or what we may wish them to represent. This external-ization of what one could term the super-ego, or conscience, then comes back to haunt us in a similar fashion to other objects that are or have been able to arouse guilt, discomfort, or feelings of inadequacy, and are thus capable of predisposing us to a host of potential persecutory anxieties. If we are being screened by an anonymous other then we may fear the discovery of parts of ourselves which we may believe to be shameful, humiliating, or perverse. The examining other may be perceived as preventing our progress and development, or, if our envy is a source of too great a discomfort and needs to be projected, they may be viewed as having the task of ensuring that we are excluded from the privileges which passing the examination has to offer; we may then believe that our success will threaten the position or standing of the examiner. The anonymous examiner behind the examination paper then becomes out to get us: an educational bouncer.

Examinations can therefore represent both the sum total of our projections, and as objects of transference re-evoke previous experi-ences of being scrutinized, judged, accepted or rejected. The demand to sit examinations may even be an outrageous assault on the self: the student who continually balks at examinations may well be the student who magically assumes that they are beyond being examined. We ought to be able to graduate without passing examinations; to be asked to perform is an insult to one's narcissism. 'They' should know how good we are without demanding proof.

It may also be that some forms of examination anxiety show a predisposition to being gender-specific. Whether that goes some way to explain the discrepancy in performance between male and female students, particularly in final examinations in higher education, is open to question, but from a psychoanalytic point of view, it cannot be denied that men and women are likely to have the potential to perceive the symbolism of examinations in ways that may be a reflection of their anatomical and biological differences. It is perhaps a curious coincidence that the academic year in higher education is generally nine months long, which for female students may well bring with it a certain perception, if not anxiety, about what it is that is gestating during this period, as well as whether what is produced will be acceptable and accepting. If what is produced in the examination is the result of nine months' gestation, then in a similar way to how women who give birth to babies are confronted with both being mothers and having to identify with their own mothers, the issue of success in examinations will necessarily lead the female examinee to have to confront the idea of being more or less successful than her mother. A corollary would be a fear of what has been growing inside one over this nine month period and whether at the end of the period one wishes to retain or expel it. This might involve separating from something which is of value.

The male equivalent may well revolve around issues of potency, performing in a circumscribed time, and 'putting pen to virgin paper' (Wooster, 1986). Triumphalist feelings may be evoked by success, (despite anticipatory fears that success may involve one's potency being stolen from one) as can post-examination reverie or depression. Failure or its anticipation may seriously question the male student's perception of his masculinity; it can represent a symbolic castration or lack of potency which may be reflected in many forms of male examination anxiety. Fantasies about what is inside us may lead us to either prematurely expel it (and one wonders just how many cases of students answering more questions than requested in an examination can be traced back to this anxiety) or to grudgingly hold on to it (answering fewer questions than required, which may also have as its genesis fantasies of a certain form of perfection).

If, as psychoanalysis would seem to suggest, anxiety can be displaced from something sexual on to something intellectual, the idea of being 'subject to examination' is intimately linked to knowledge, curiosity, and by implication, sexuality. In this context it is interesting to note that the Victorians believed that the failure to pass an examination was a result of excessive masturbation. If we assume that a certain form of examination anxiety can be a displacement from the realm of sexuality to the realm of intellect, then any examination will leave us open to anxieties, not merely about competence and adequacy, but whether the process will involve an enrichment or depletion. The pleasure at passing may conversely increase anxiety about a catastrophic loss in the future; at least if we fail we have, metaphorically, nothing to lose.

Becoming a student in higher education carries with it the implication that one is joining an elite group and leaving behind those less advantaged, who may subsequently come to be viewed as weak, and, as a result, denigrated. Joining an elite and idealized group allows one to identify with the qualities associated with that particular group, such as superiority or denigration of others, while less comforting traits can safely be left behind in those who are viewed as having not succeeded. Thus on entering higher education we may feel we have left behind certain of our less attractive traits; vulnerability, confusion, helplessness, which are carried by those excluded from a university education. However, examinations will always confront us as a result of our possible failure with the danger of having to re-incorporate those traits which we thought were securely placed in others. Just when we thought we had jettisoned discomforting parts of ourselves, examinations ensure that they may come back to haunt us. There is a certain inevitability about this since it is difficult to pass every examination, including the subjective tests that we set ourselves. Additionally, those designated by us as failures may prove unwilling to passively accept their projected fate.

Examination success carries with it the ever-present danger of a certain experience of fraudulence: how can we ever be sure we really passed?

> An eminent and successful man in his 40s, remembered a recurring dream in which he dreamt that while still at school he had failed one of his A-level examinations, which would mean he would have to return to the same school the following year to re-sit the examination, instead of leaving school. The dream suggested that his return would be in his 40-year-old body. Aside from the suggested regressive wish, and the fact that A-levels had come at a particularly sensitive time in his life, the central facet of this dream was – despite this man's eminence in an academic field and the fact that he had passed this particular A-level with the highest possible grade – the disturbing suggestion that he would be found out and exposed as an impostor. Consciously, during this man's waking life, he felt both competent and able, but his dream suggested otherwise.

Is it possible to dream about failing an examination without first having passed the examination in real life? And if not, why should those who have been successful in examinations be constantly vulnerable to recurring examination-anxiety dreams associated with examination failure? It is a curious paradox that these dreams tend to be dreamt by seemingly successful people, who have nothing, or everything, to lose. Does examination success increase our vulnerability to fears of both fraudulence and exposure? In some real sense we are all imposters constantly in danger of being found out. Our recurring nightmares of confronting the test and failing, suggest that despite our manifest attainments we can never fully believe in our successes or rid ourselves of the suspicion that they might prove illusory and be magically taken away from us. Does success estrange us from our true selves? In Ingmar Bergman's film 'Wild Strawberries' there is a scene in which an eminent professor, shortly before receiving a great academic honour, dreams the night before the ceremony, of failing an examination. Fraudulence stalks us. It may well be that our true selves are rather shameful and insignificant, and that our achievements are at some level never experienced as fully authentic. The brittle quality of our success may well be linked in some fashion to the distinction between our true and false selves. Where the latter becomes too distant from the former, not least in terms of examination honours, we are always in danger of being found wanting, or even imploding on ourselves. Because we have all been children, and consequently always vulnerable to the thought that adults know best, or are doing it properly, we can never quite free ourselves from childlike preoccupations.

> Everyone who has passed the matriculation examination at the end of his school studies complains of the obstinacy with which he is pursued by anxiety dreams of having failed, or of being obliged to take the examination again, etc. In the case of those who have obtained a university degree this typical dream is replaced by another one which represents them as having failed their university finals; and it is in vain that they object, even while they are still asleep, that for years they have been practising medicine or working as university lecturers or heads of offices. The ineradicable memories of the punishments that we suffered for our evil deeds in childhood become active within us once more and attach themselves to . . . our stiffest examinations (Freud, 1900).

Freud reflects on the possibility that only people who had in fact passed these examinations dreamt these dreams, and speculates on whether, given that these dreams were generally dreamt the night before a further test, they represented an attempt by the dreamer to undo any possible anxiety about the forthcoming event. We are also, he implies, in danger of constantly being punished for our childhood vices. What could they be? Hubris for being so bold as to desire or contemplate and believe in our ambitious selves? Janine Chasseguet-Smirgel (1985) commenting on the fact that examinations often occur at transition points in a child's life, suggests that examination dreams emphasize the 'gap between the true age' of the dreamer (and the fact that the examination has been passed), with the often, childlike, or childish, anxiety expressed in the dream. The function of the dream is then to correct, adjust or repair perceived gaps in our development. Their aim is a form of integration which, despite outward appearances, the dreamer unconsciously questions.

A feeling of deceit, or a certain lack of internal coherence, will lead us to continually dream the dream again, for we can never rid ourselves of the suspicion that we obtained the qualification without truly deserving it. The internal examiner, albeit externalized, is a severe and unrelenting taskmaster:

Eric was a highly-strung, androgynous, vain young student who initially sought help as a result of increasing concern about his physical appearance; he was troubled by a temporary facial disfigurement, and obtained no relief from the assurance that this was a transitory ailment. He came from a family which had experienced considerable disharmony, including the separation and remarriage of both parents when Eric was still quite young. He had always been relentlessly competitive, and shone in all fields: as well as being academically successful he was also a gifted sportsman, singer and actor. He loved acting and would obtain great satisfaction from appearing on stage, knowing all his lines, and inviting as well as receiving the admiration of his audience. Facial 'spottiness' was clearly a problem, and although not immediately noticeable, Eric felt that everyone could see his 'blemish' which led him to forget his lines and, in his eyes at least, to give a determinedly poor performance. The audience would be shocked, expecting much greater things of him. Similarly, in his first examination 'performance' at university which pitted him against other able students, he metaphorically forgot his lines, became overwhelmed with anxiety at the thought that his unseen examiners would view him as less than brilliant, broke down in tears and left the examination hall in the middle of the examination. For the first time he feared others would see and experience him as flawed as he experienced and saw himself. As compensation for his disrupted and traumatic childhood, he had turned himself into what he believed was the object of envy: others envied his brilliance, including his capacity to sail through examinations and his good looks. Consequently, he needed to set himself unrealistic and unattainable high standards for fear that should he fall short of these goals he would no longer be enviable. His facial rash spurred him on to want to attain ever greater heights which, even when achieved, led him to feel uneasy since these accomplishments could in no way compensate for his facial disfigurement, which, as far as he was concerned, existed for the whole world to see.

Where the dominant motivational force behind success is to evoke envy in others, we can always be brought short by our own imperfections. An additional worrying aspect of Eric's problem was his compulsive need to scratch his blemish, which had the effect of exacerbating his imperfection. From a psychological point of view this could be seen as an attempt by Eric to explore the part of himself which was felt to be less than perfect. No matter how successful we are we remain both curious about, and at times fatally attracted to, our own shortcomings. Examinations confront us with a dilemma: success may invite feelings of self-sufficiency or perfection bringing with it fears of isolation, while failure may confront us with the terror of our own helplessness and vulnerability leading to a fear of loss of autonomy. The truth about the self is that it is brittle; examination success can give a false coherence to the idea of a self. If the sense of self is in essence illusory, then examination success would serve to consolidate an illusion. A fear of failure may be linked to a fear of failing to have meaning. If tests question our notion of self, the self then becomes that which is constituted by the test. Consequently, if our sense of self is validated by the test, then the question becomes: What is it in ourselves that needs and seeks validation and qualification? It is in this context that the 'test' is so ambivalently sought, and so difficult to relinquish, particularly if we have been informed that we passed.

Conclusion

In order to have one's vocation recognised, three conditions had to be fulfilled: it must have been apparent since childhood; must have been successfully thwarted by parents, school and environment; must have emerged more urgent than ever, reinforced by all the frustrations and obstacles . . . (Pontalis, 1993).

Writing this book has from time to time appeared replete with frustrations and obstacles. In attempting to convey the variety of our subjective agendas I have had to face the nature of mine in undertaking to explore and link education and psychoanalysis. The obstacles experienced on the way have, with hindsight, been turning-points in the book's development.

Psychoanalysis can help us decode symptoms. I hope that this book has demonstrated how analytic concepts assist us in understanding the complex nature of what we want from and what is demanded of us by education. Education and psychoanalysis have almost in tandem moved from an aesthetic of desire to one of nurture. It is as if we are forced as teachers, students, or therapists to choose between the two. Bipolar models, which as we have seen are ubiquitous, demand that we choose between opposites. In psychoanalysis this goes back to Freud's differentiation between the ego and the id; one being integrated and rational while the other a mass of chaotic and unformed passion. This made possible other splits, signifying reason and emotion which, in an applied form, now permeate our thinking in education. Intellect and feelings, mind and body, male and female, 'hard' and 'soft' subjects, and the division between examinations and continual assessment are examples of this polarization. The point in Freud's initial dichotomy, which is in danger of being lost, is that a relationship exists between these two opposites. The ego cannot function without the id, and vice versa. What is important is the relationship that is established between the two, the process of how these apparently irreconcilable opposites negotiate their differences and the obstacles that are encountered on the way.

I hope that this book, in attempting to think about education from a psychoanalytic framework, has shed some light on the nature of those processes and the obstacles to an approach which seeks to integrate the seemingly opposite. The function of splitting is to manage, if not deny, difference. The subjective curriculum suggests that we learn with our emotions as well as our minds. It is the interaction of the two which significantly affects our educational scripts. Since both education and psychoanalysis are at best about exploring the nature of difference, both can optimally teach us something about valuing difference rather than colonizing sameness. We remain at best ambivalent about, at worst disturbed by, difference in our society and are tempted to find ways to control difference by normative and adaptive therapies and a structured and hierarchical educational system whose goal is increasingly homogeneity.

> Goddess of bossy underlings, Normality!
> What murders are committed in thy name!
> Totalitarian is thy state Reality,
> Reeking of antiseptics and the shame
> Of faces that all look and feel the same.
> Thy Muse is one unknown to classic histories,
> The topping figure of the hockey mistress.
>
> I hate the modern trick, to tell the truth,
> Of straightening out the kinks in the young mind,
> Our passion for the tender plant of youth,
> Our hatred for all weeds of any kind.
> Slogans are bad: the best that I can find
> Is this: 'Let each child have that's in our care
> As much neurosis as the child can bear.'
>
> W.H. Auden, 'Letter to Lord Byron', 1938

Bibliography

Auden, W.H. 'Letter to Lord Byron', *Letters from Iceland*, Auden and Macniece. Faber & Faber, 1938.

Benjamin, J. *Psychoanalysis, Feminism and the Problem of Domination*. Virago Press, 1990.

Berry Brazelton, T. and Cramer, B.G. *The Earliest Relationship: Parents, Infants and the Drama of Early Attachment*. Karnac Books, 1991.

Bernheimer, C. and Kahane, C. *In Dora's Case: Freud, Hysteria, Feminism*. Virago Press, 1985.

Bion, W.R. *Second Thoughts*. Karnac Books, 1990

Bloss, P. *On Adolescence*. New York, Free Press, 1962.

——*The Adolescent Passage*. New York University Press, 1979.

Bollas, C. *The Shadow of the Object: Psychoanalysis and the Unthought Known*. Free Association Books, 1987.

Bringuier, J. *Conversations with Jean Piaget*. Chicago University Press, 1980.

Campbell, D. and Hale, R. 'Suicidal Acts', in *Textbook of Psychotherapy in Psychiatric Practice*. Holmes, J. (ed.). Churchill Livingstone, 1991.

Chasseguet-Smirgel, J. *Creativity and Perversion*. Free Association Books, 1985, pp. 30–35.

Chodorow, N. *The Reproduction of Mothering*. Berkeley, University of California Press, 1978.

Deutsch, H. *Neurosis and Character Types*. International University Press, 1965.

Erikson, E. 'The problem of Ego Identity', in *Journal of American Psychoanalysis* (4). 1956.

——*Identity: Youth and Crisis*. New York, W.W. Norton, 1968.

——*Childhood and Society*. Triad/Granada, 1977.

Freud, A. *Psychoanalysis for Teachers and Parents*. Norton, 1955.

——'Adolescence', in *Psychoanalytic Study of the Child*, vol. 13: pp. 255–78, 1958.

Freud, S. *The Interpretation of Dreams*. S.E. IV and V. London, Hogarth Press, 1900, pp. 337–380.

——*The Psychopathology of Everyday Life*. S.E. vol. VI. 1901.

——*Three Essays on the Theory of Sexuality*. S.E. vol. XI. 1905.

——*An Open Letter to Dr. M. Furst*. S.E. vol. IX. 1907, pp. 129–139.

——*Analysis of a Phobia in a Five-Year-Old Boy*. S.E. vol. XI. 1909, p.145.

——*Formulations of the Two Principles of Mental Functioning*. S.E.

vol. XII 1912, pp. 213–226.

——*Some Reflections on Schoolboy Psychology*. S.E. vol. XIII. 1914, pp. 241–244.

——*Mourning and Melancholia*. S.E. vol. XIV. 1917, pp. 237–258.

——*Femininity* S.E. vol. XXII. 1933, p.116.

——Introduction to Aichorn, A. *Wayward Youth*. Putnam, 1936.

——*Autobiographical Study*. Hogarth Press, 1946.

Herzen, A. *Childhood, Youth and Exile*. World's Classics, 1994.

Higher Education Quarterly. Spring, 1987.

Hinshelwood, R. D. *A Dictionary of Kleinian Thought*. Free Association Books, 1989.

Inhelder, S. and Piaget, J. *The Growth of Logical Thinking*. Routledge, 1958.

Illich, I. *Deschooling Society*. Calder and Boyars, 1971.

Jones, E. 'Some Problems of Adolescence', in *Papers on Psychoanalysis*. Ballière, Tindall-Cox, 1948.

Jones, R. *Fantasy and Feeling in Education*. New York University Press, 1968.

Keller, E. *Reflections on Gender and Science*. Yale University Press, 1985.

Khan, M. 'Infantile Neurosis as a False Self Organisation', in *Privacy of the Self*. The International Psycho-analytic Library, Hogarth Press, 1974.

Klein, M. 'The Role of the School in the Libidinal Development of the Child', 1923.

——'The importance of Symbol Formation in the Development of the Ego', 1930.

——'A Contribution to the Theory of Intellectual Inhibition', 1931, all in *The Writings of Melanie Klein, Vol. 1*. Hogarth, 1975.

——'The Psychoanalysis of Children.' Hogarth, 1931.

Lasch, C. *The Culture of Narcissism*. New York, Norton, 1979.

——*The Minimal Self: Psychic Survival in Troubled Times*. New York, Norton, 1984.

Laufer, M. and M.E. *Adolescence and Developmental Breakdown: A Psychoanalytic View*. Yale University Press, 1984.

Mahler, M. *et al. The Psychological Birth of the Human Infant*. New York, Basic Books, 1975.

Marias, J. *All Souls*. Harvill, 1989.

McDougall, J. *Theatres of the Body*. Norton, 1989.

Meltzer, D. 'Pedagogic Implications of Structural Psychosexual Theory', in *Sexual States of Mind*. Clunie Press, 1973.

——'Identification and Socialisation in Adolescence', Chapter 7, in *Sexual States of Mind*.

Menzies-Lyth, I. *Containing Anxiety in Institutions: Selected Essays*. Free Association Books, 1988.

——*The Dynamics of the Social: Selected Essays.* Free Association Books, 1989.

Orbach, S. *Hunger Strike.* Virago, 1993.

Phillips, A. *Winnicott.* Fontana Press, 1988.

——'Looking at Obstacles', Chapter 8, in *On Kissing, Tickling and Being Bored.* Faber and Faber, 1993.

——'On Success', in *On Flirtation.* Faber and Faber, 1994.

Pontalis, J.B. *Love of Beginnings.* Free Association Books, 1993.

Popper, K. 'The Bucket and the Searchlight: Two Theories of Knowledge' in *Objective Knowledge: An Evolutionary Approach.* Oxford, The Clarendon Press, 1972.

Riviere, J. 'Womanliness as a masquerade', in *The International Journal of Psychoanalysis*, 9, pp.303–313. 1929.

Roth, P. *Patrimony: A True Story.* Jonathan Cape, 1991.

Salzberger-Wittenberg, I. *et al. The Emotional Experience of Learning and Teaching.* Routledge, 1983.

Stern, D. *The Interpersonal World of the Infant: A View from Developmental Psychology.* Basic Books, 1985.

Symington, N. *Narcissism: a New Theory.* Karnac Books, 1993.

Vienna Psychoanalytic Society. *1910 Discussions of the Vienna Psychoanalytic Society: On Suicide with particular reference to suicide amongst Young Students.* International University Press, 1967.

Winnicott, D. 'Aggression in relation to emotional development', in *Collected Papers: Through Paediatrics to Psychoanalysis.* Tavistock, 1953; New York, Basic Books, 1958.

——*The International Journal of Psychoanalysis.* vol. XXIV, 34, p.97. 1953.

——'Transitional Objects and Transitional Phenomena' in *Collected Papers: Through Paediatrics to Psycho-analysis.* 1958.

——'Ego Distortion in terms of True and False Self', in *The Maturational Process and the Facilitating Environment: Studies in the Theory of Emotional Development.* Hogarth Press, 1965.

——*The Child, the Family, and the Outside World.* Harmondsworth, Penguin, 1964.

——'Communicating and not Communicating Leading to a Study of Certain Opposites', in *The Maturational Process and the Facilitating Environment: Studies in the Theory of Emotional Development.* Hogarth Press and The Institute of Psycho-analysis, 1965.

——*Playing and Reality.* Tavistock, 1972.

——*Babies and their Mothers.* Free Association Books, 1988.

Wittenberg, I. et al. *The Emotional Experience of Learning and Teaching.* Routledge, 1983.

Wooster, G. 'Working psychotherapeutically in a student health setting', in *Psychoanalytic Psychotherapy*, Vol. 2 No. 2. pp.111–121, 1986.

| *Index*